Moments

Life, Romance and Spiritual Reflection

ISBN: 978-1-105-64059-9

By: Thayer Alden Smith

Aka; Professor 929

ISBN: 978-1-105-64059-9

®

Please visit www.professor929.com for information on upcoming events and other details related to this book. Thank you.

Table of Contents

Romance

Commentary

Spiritual

Foreword:

Social commentary is a privilege that many of our sisters and brothers do not have. In many lands the freedom to speak is suppressed by means of physical violence and even pain of death. So, finding myself living in a relatively free society, I feel compelled to speak out about my passions. I do not hold back, because I consider the potential good my words can bring by inspiring those who may feel as I do. If nothing else, I have found writing to be therapeutic. Writing has proven to be a vehicle, which allows me to travel to the inner most reaches of my heart and my mind, and discover the man within.

This is a collection of poems, which I started in the summer of 2009 with the exception of 'The Outer Edge', which I wrote in 1988. I simply poured out my heart and the words took their form on the paper. I hope you enjoy these poems. It is with the deepest sincerity that they were created. It is with the greatest humility that I present them for your consideration.

Thank you,

P-929

Appreciation:

I thank the Creator who makes all things possible. It is also important for me to take the time to thank my Mother, who taught me a keen appreciation for art in all of its' many forms. I thank you Mom, for providing a sanctuary for my thoughts and dreams. I thank my Father for being wise enough to not only share with me his successes, but also his failures. To my older brother Thane, I thank you for showing me The Way. To my best friend Bruce, I would like to thank you for hanging in there with me through thick and through thin. You're a hell of a man, but you're always my boy! To Carl, thank you for "inciting a riot"! To Dr. Bogan and his wife Carol, *The Miracle Worker*, thank you for believing in me.

I thank my two beautiful daughters, Briana & Siani, for teaching me about life, and helping me to grow into the happy man I have become. I thank you Rob, for the good times we had when we were young.

To my younger brother Eldon, I am overjoyed that you have re-entered my life. I have missed you deeply, and look forward to making up for lost time.

I thank you Brandi, for melting my frozen heart, and nurturing my wounded soul. Your tender affection and undying optimism are as essential to me as the air that I breathe. To me, you represent all that is good in life. To me, you epitomize hope. I'll love you forever!

I do not believe that this collection would exist if not for each of you working your magic in my life!

Much love,

P-929

Dedication

Thomas Harris Smith Jr. 1961, Benjamin Franklin High School, Philadelphia, PA

I dedicate this collection of poems to the late great Thomas Harris Smith Jr.; a man who entered this world with nothing and yet departed with everything. He was my father, my mentor, my chief consigliore and my very best friend.

> *"I will not despair*
> *My kindhearted friend*
> *For I know in my heart that I'll see you again"*

A word from the Author:

It is my sincere hope that you enjoy this collection of poems I have assembled for your consideration.

The Fairer Sex

Many of my poems are about women. Women are beautifully intriguing enchanted creatures. Unfortunately, they are terribly misunderstood by men in general. It has occurred to me that to truly begin to understand a woman, you must first embrace women as a whole, as well as on an individual basis. I do not claim to understand women. However, I am learning a great deal from the fairer sex because I have learned how to listen. Women are wonderful teachers if you allow them to teach. They are also wonderful students if you just give them a chance to learn. Honesty is required, raw, naked honesty! Don't be afraid. Give it a chance.

At any rate, I will continue to write about women because they are intellectually fascinating and artistically beautiful.

Warrior

Many of my poems discuss the nuances of war. Ironically, I do not believe in war. However, I do believe in the warrior. Real warriors adhere to a code. In the truest tradition, a warrior is one who protects those who cannot protect themselves. This is an honorable tradition. It epitomizes the very essence of altruism. One who would sacrifice himself for the good of his fellowman is truly heroic. Warriors are greater than the sum of their training and weapons. Warrior is a state of the mind and of the heart. The best warriors exist to preserve life not end it. I encourage you to have an honest conversation with a seasoned warrior. You may learn something about both life and death.

Faith

As you consider this collection you may notice that a number of poems take on a spiritual tone. As irony would have it, it would appear that the unseen elements of the universe are the most "real", and therefore, possess a certain permanence about them. Conversely, life has taught me that the tangibles of life often prove to be the most transient. In my humble opinion I believe that the Bible captures this concept best in the book of Hebrews in chapter 11. In light of this, I often find that my thoughts center on matters of faith. I hold faith dear. As fragile as faith may be, it can make us invincible in the crucible of life.

Structure

This book is actually six books in one. Thus, the main body of work is separated into six sections:

- Reflection

- Warrior

- Sentiments

- Commentary

- Spiritual

- Romance

Each poem within a particular section adheres to a central theme. However, Sentiments is really two themes in one. The first being poems of inspiration. The second being poems of tribute. Additionally, I have attempted to arrange the collection in such a way that tells a story about life in general. I do hope that you enjoy this collection.

Reflection

"The end is a blessing
To settle all debt
At the end there's no pain, no toil, no sweat"

Time

Time is the predator
Searching for prey
Hunting us all day after day

Relentless by nature
Persistent and true
Looking for me, looking for you

You can't out run it
You cannot hide
Time is never on anyone's side

The hands never rest
On your wristwatch or clock
Constantly moving a tick for a tock

No rest for the weary
Till the end of their time
But your end and his end do not equal mine

It whittles down mountains
And displaces seas
Time breaks your body just like a disease

We have to accept it
Can't hold it at bay
Time rules your night, time runs your day

But you cannot have music
Without keeping time
Time keeps the beat that goes with the rhyme

Perhaps, time's a tool
To master with ease
To pilot the planes and navigate seas

Perhaps, time's not evil
It's misunderstood
Time can be used wisely. Perhaps, time is good

- Professor 929

The End

At the end of the road
At the end of the day
At the end of the week we receive our pay

At the end of the story
There is always a prize
At the end of the night there is always sunrise

To the ends of the earth
We go on a quest
At the end of the journey there is always a rest

The end is a blessing
To settle all debt
At the end there's no pain, no toil, no sweat

At the end of the end
There's no losing or winning
But there's always hope of a bright new beginning

At the end of it all
We run out of time
And now we have come to the end of this rhyme

The End

- Professor 929

Twilight

Here in the twilight
Possessed by malaise
I sit in the garden reviewing the days

Once a young fellow
Now I am old
Lusting for warmth yet fettered by cold

I've had a full life
I dare not complain
My friends are all gone and yet I remain

I've seen many things
I've been many places
I've learned a great deal in wide open spaces

I have survived
Though I do not know how
I've had more fun than the law should allow

I've lived a life
With little regret
A life time of memories I shall not forget!

I've loved a good woman
For most of my life
Compassionate lover, companion and wife

Joy of my heart
My children have grown
With families and interests and minds of their own

Winter upon me
I'm rested at last
The time for adventure and conquest has passed

Pleased with the days
In the twilight of years
Embracing tomorrow without any fears

-Professor 929

Change

Change is a constant
I know it sounds strange
Change is a freight train that will not be changed

Change has been dreaded
By those at the top
Change is a force that no one can stop

Change can work for you
So please do not fear
Change is adventure; a brand new frontier

I will embrace change
Without any regret
Change will be changing that is a sure bet!

Change is a teacher
By now we should know
Change is the magic that helps us to grow

Let's all grow together
Leave your worries behind
All that you need is a flexible mind

Change is approaching
It's coming today
It will run you over. Don't stand in the way!

Change has arrived
A new day has begun
So let it be written. So let it be done!

I will get onboard
I do comprehend
I so love adventure. I'll make change my friend!

- Professor 929

Life

We live for the future
Yet dwell in the past
We realize our years have flown by much too fast

Frantically fighting
For our daily bread
Feeding our families and getting ahead

Insatiable visions
Of fortune and fame
We scarcely have time to enjoy the game

Life is the game
We play and pursue
Though sometimes you must let the game come to you

Our days are a gift
Can't be bought or sold
Unwrap them with care, let each one unfold

Savor the moment
A complex bouquet
Immersing yourself in the joys of the day

You've earned your reward
With the sweat of your brow
Get lost for a time in the art of the now

Life is a banquet
With family and friends
Relish each bite before the meal ends

Life is a rhythm
A beautiful song
Life, like a river, keeps rolling along

- Professor 929

War

The spilling of blood
Seems futile to me
Fighting and killing just should not be

Are we not brothers?
No matter the season
Can't we negotiate? Why can we not reason?

Did you just say?
You won't talk anymore?
You have decided we must go to war?

We can't trust some leaders
It's quite plain to see
The power of peace lies with you and with me

We must stop the killing
If only we could
We might pursue peace in a way that is good

It's not hard
To understand
Extending some love to your fellow man

So, what if we reason
With those over seas
Invite them to sit down and talk if they please

Does that make us weak?
I just don't see how
It's somewhat like beating your swords into ploughs

If we carefully listen
I'm certain we'll learn
About our new friend, their respect we might earn

I'm sure they have some things
Which they value high
If we just get to know them no one has to die

Could we be so different?
From our fellow man
I'm sure they have laughter in far away lands

Humor might work
Maybe laughter's the key
If we laugh, and they laugh, it might help us to see

That we're just not that different
Hey, how does this sound?
Perhaps we could try to find some common ground

Embrace our dear neighbor
Just think of his mom
We won't be so quick to use bullets and bombs

If we show true love
Death just might be cheated
Treat them in way that we want to be treated

We should realize
That we all should be friends
We must take a stand. The killing must end!

- Professor 929

Peace

Peace is a bird
Elusive and free
Peace is a picture that some cannot see

Peace needs nurturing
That it might grow
Peace won't survive with the status quo

Open your heart
Unclench your fist
Extending your hand for peace to exist

Peace gives us hope
For something to reach
Peace is essential for freedom of speech

Peace is a vision
All people should see
It's better for you, it's better for me

- Professor 929

Words

I love to write
Whenever I can
Always with pencil and paper in hand

Sculpting in words
My latest desire
Lately my pencil has been on fire!

Incessantly scribbling
Phrases and blurbs
Painting these pictures with all of these words

Free to express
Whatever I feel
The power to wound, the power to heal

The power to reach
Across space and time
That power is yours, that power is mine

Reporting to others
Is what I might do
I see the story and tell it to you

Writing the truth
Is better for me
Help giving others the power to see

- Professor 929

Flame

Such a free spirit
Rash and untamed
You dance as you flicker
You are my friend Flame

Deeply hypnotic
With an ambient glow
You become stronger
As the winds start to blow

Ever insatiable
You grow as you eat
For the more you consume
The greater your heat

You whisper sweet nothings
As you wistfully speak
I start to let go
As you sing me to sleep

You do cook my meals
And power my car
I fear without you
I wouldn't get far

I can't live without you
I need you each day
You light up my life
And you keep cold away

So, I will keep you close
And remember your name
You are quite a character
You are my friend Flame

- Professor 929

Speed

Speed is my vice
I live by the wheel
For the faster I go, the better I feel

Pushing the limits
I'm doing just fine
While shredding the track on my 929

A twist of the wrist
As I lean in the turn
My heart starts to race, as I smell rubber burn

I kick the rear out
Ever so slight
My knees grip the tank balanced and tight

I drive a fine line
I'm steady of nerve
So, I roll on the gas as I exit the curve

I'm in a zone now
The warm-up is done
Man and machine have just become one

My worries behind me
My stress is all gone
I smile as the revs sing a symphonic song

As the sun sets
I turn on my lights
I keep right on shredding into the night

I click off the laps
Again and again
Riding this rocket's outrageously Zen

I just can't get enough!
For I still feel the need
So, I give her more gas, and she gives me more speed!

- Professor 929

Conversation

The art of conversation
Is now all but extinct
Interactions now are absent depth and very much succinct

Prisoners of our culture
We often seem to be
Let's rise above this madness and endeavor to be free

Unplug from your devices
Stretch your legs to walk
Reconnect with people. Take the time to talk

By learning one another
We'll form a tighter bond
We'll stroll a path together and take our friendship far beyond

Let's sit down for a moment
And share that cup of tea
Let's take time to enjoy one another's company

I value your opinion
And the thoughts expressed by you
Even if we disagree I see your point of view

Conversation is a story
Intriguing as it's told
Just melt into the moment and let dialogue unfold

Discussion is the key
To the knowledge that we seek
You too will impart knowledge in the wisdom that you speak

The art of conversation
Rediscovered by a few
Conversation you're a treasure, perhaps there's hope for you

- Professor 929

Be

I sometimes wonder
If I were not me
Would I exist, would I still be?

Further I ponder
If I were to be
But I was not me, what would I see?

What would I think?
What would I feel?
Would I still dream, would my world seem as real?

How would I look?
What tongue would I speak?
Would I be bold or humble and meek?

Would I be rich?
Would I be poor?
Would my path be certain, or somewhat obscure?

The things I believe
The things that I say
Would I see these things quite the same way?

Where am I going?
Where am I from?
What are the chapters still yet to come?

What of my future?
Can I be sure?
Have I ever been by this way before?

I am that I am
It's great to be me
Life is a treasure. I'm grateful to be.

- Professor 929

Cro-Magnon Man

I'm Cro-Magnon Man
I don't cry or sing
You must understand it's a Cro-Magnon thing

I eat red meat
I hunt with a knife
I live to the full everyday of my life

My body is strong
My hide is thick
I 'm out in the cold and I never get sick

Deep in the wilds
With trees all around
My knuckles are raw from dragging the ground

Heart of a lion
Soul of a ram
Glorious, primitive beast of a man

Your world is obtuse
I'll never conform
The "men" of today cannot weather the storm

Afraid to step up
To utter the truth
You're trained to be weak from the time of your youth

You don't respect women
You will never win
You have never learned what it means to be men

Evolve into men
I know that you can
Take it from me, I'm Cro-Magnon Man

- Professor 929

Circus

Circus music
Is what I hear
Barnum and Bailey all in my ear

Every day is a circus
Some ridiculous test
Some lions and tigers and you know the rest

Problems mounting
At a dizzying pace
There's chaos and carnage all over the place

I can take it
I won't quiver or shake
I may bend a little, but I'm not going to break

Come on inside
There's no place to hide
The center ring is where I reside

I stay on task
Just holding it down
I do not have time for clowning around

I'm getting too old
For this kind of crap
I jump in, I get down and then it's a wrap

Problems solved
Fires put out
I come out on top with never a doubt

I'm good to go
So send in the clowns
It's always a blast with the circus in town

- Professor 929

First Date

Hello, do come in
Glad to meet you young man
My daughter's not ready. So, tell me your plans

Come on now please tell me
There's no need for fears
Feel free to speak up; in fact, I'm all ears

I know you'll behave
On your very first date
I don't want to hurt you so, don't stay out too late

Ok, I am sorry
That's really not true
To be perfectly honest, I'd love to harm you!

In fact, let me say
If you act like a pig
I'll snap you in two just like a dry twig!

I'll work you real good
With a torch and a saw
You'll be eating your meals through a clear plastic straw!

And you better not touch her!
Keep your hands to yourself
Or I'll beat you real good with that club on the shelf

Please understand
I just do not play
Hear my words clearly. I mean what I say!

And you still won't be safe
When I go to jail
I'll find you my friend 'cause' my wife will post bail!

That's a definite son
I didn't say maybe
I'll plant you in the ground and I'll sleep like a baby.

Oh, her she comes
Doesn't she look great?
Hope you two enjoy your very first date.

Help

Help me I've fallen
And I can't get back up
I struggle to live but I just self-destruct

This monster's too big
For me to defeat
Alone and dejected my failure's complete

Will someone please help me?
Cause I am fading fast
I fear without help I just will not last

The blows are now coming
In rapid succession
I just cannot make it without your protection

So I'm begging you brother
Please lend me a hand
If you let me lean on you I know I can stand

Please don't wait and do nothing
Standing idly by
If you'd get involved I won't have to die

I was once a strong man
With plenty of wealth
Though today I can't seem to take care of myself

Come rescue me brother
I have faith in you
I dare not loose hope. I know you'll come through

- Professor 929

Darkness

Alone in the darkness
Shallow of breath
I take a few moments to contemplate death

The ultimate thief
It robs us of life
Losing our friends spawns anguish and strife

Don't let death deceive you
In times of self-doubt
In times of despair it can seem a way out

To take your own life
Is a horrible sin
Don't go down that path, it's just a dead end

Come walk with me brother
We'll work it all out
Together we'll see what this troubles' about

Take care of yourself
Live well and stay strong
Your loved ones will miss you one day when you're gone

But dearly beloved
We're gathered today
To celebrate life, and keep death at bay

- Professor 929

Cry

Cry for the babies
In a far away land
Wanting of food and empty of hand

Cry for the widow
Who is walking alone
Broken of heart and brittle of bone

Cry for the soldier
With secrets to keep
Haunted, tortured and wanting of sleep

Cry for the mother
With a troubled child
Destructive, hopeless , needy and wild

Cry for the father
Who's lost his son
Needlessly killed at the end of a gun

Cry for the poor
With nothing to eat
Homeless, hungry and out on the street

Cry for the innocent
Locked in a cell
Without a hope and living in hell

Cry for the many
Sins of the past
Pray for the broken, the sick and down cast

Pray for tomorrow
An end to all fears
An end to all sorrows, weeping and tears

- Professor 929

Fear

Fear is a plague
On the whole of mankind
Fear is a dungeon of the heart and the mind

Fear is a weapon
To control the meek
It drains us of life so we become weak

Fear will infect you
And rip out your spine
Fear will keep you from holding the line

Panic and fright
Is a price that we pay
Fear can kill you a little each day

Terror will torment
The unshielded soul
Fear will keep you from reaching your goal

It can paralyze
Or so it would seem
Fear will keep you from living your dream

Fear is a wall
It won't block my way
Fear is a dragon that I mean to slay

Truth is the power
Setting me free
The more that I learn, the more I can see

I shall not relent
As danger draws near
As time passes on I'll conquer my fear

- Professor 929

Pain

Pain: A companion
I'd rather not have
When he's here for a visit I'm dreadfully sad

Whenever he comes
He's never invited
The thought of him leaving makes me real excited

He wrinkles my face
And attacks my bones
I truly wish pain would just leave me alone

I'd take my prescription
And tell pain good bye
But lately the prices have been way too high

Quite a decision
My meds or my heat
And I just can't survive without something to eat

I guess he'll be staying
This miserable pest
Pain is the rudest unwelcome houseguest

I'll tell you, I hate pain!
Now and again
He's always around, but he's never my friend

- Professor 929

Treacherous Heart

(Jeremiah 17:9)

Deceitful by nature
Failing to show it
The heart is treacherous. Who can know it?

Proving disloyal
Time after time
Possessing no logic nor reason or rhyme

Easily wounded
It struggles to heal
Painting a picture that just isn't real

Cloudy of vision
Distorting your view
Creating a world that just isn't true

The cradle of passion
That no one can trust
Desperate, wanting and driven by lust

Primitive beast
As free as a flame
The heart must be molded, sculpted and tamed

Strengthened, sharpened
Hardened like steel
Able to cope with the things that you feel

Anger, sorrow
Joy and fear
The passion for those whom you hold dear

Balanced emotion
Becomes an art
When you learn to control the treacherous heart

-Professor 929

Secrets

The keeper of secrets
Discreetly aware
Intimate truths I've chosen to bear

I hear with compassion
For I understand
So, they've chosen to place their hearts in my hand

Divulging the darkness
Is truly unjust
I'm honored to protect the sacred trust

Unfortunate aspect
Of everyone's life
Secrets can cut you as deep as a knife

They must be respect
And handled with care
A secret betrayed will bring forth despair

Out in the open
Hurting too much
Mortally wounding the lives that they touch

They must stay contained
Avoiding conflicts
No broken secret can ever be fixed

Dangerous poison
I bind them with locks
They must remain hidden entombed in a box

I'll keep all the secrets
Right down to the death
Integrity keeper to the last breath

- Professor 929

Regret

Regret is the gift
That keeps on giving
The anguish of life, I can't stop reliving

Mistakes that I've made
Long in the past
The depth of the wounds and hurts are too vast

Rampart of sadness
It stands in my way
Regret is the specter that haunts me each day

Memories that linger
As sharp as a knife
They'll plague and influence the rest of my life

Given the chance
I would change the past
The outcome would mark a dramatic contrast

I have not the power
I can't change a thing
I have to submit and live on with the sting

Mistakes are not wasted
Although without plan
They help me become a much wiser man

The errors of flesh
I've often lamented
Regrets are the sorrows I could have prevented

Regrets are a burden
My conscience the slave
Regrets are regrettable right down to the grave

The sum of all blunders
I'll never forget
The pain of the ages, the grief of regret

- Professor 929

Consequence

Consequences
For all that I do
A fact of life that's painfully true

A constant of life
That demands respect
As simple to grasp as cause and effect

It's quite inescapable
Perfectly clear
Consequences can be quite severe

The price must be paid
For actions I take
Whether intended or just a mistake

Accepting the cost
For all that I choose
Resulting in whether I win or I loose

Tenacious dilemma
I've known from the start
Consequences can rip you apart

Unmerciful teacher
As sharp as a knife
Consequences can cost you your life

A vessel of justice
Stark and austere
The lessons delivered are utterly clear

Be wise my friend
Learn from my pain
Consequences can drive you insane

-Professor 929

Pariah

I am the pariah
My intentions are good
Though it seems that I'm terribly misunderstood

The way that I'm treated
Just isn't right
The way that I'm viewed is a pitiful sight

Falsely accused
So I stand apart
Indicted by people with imperfect hearts

Blinded by pride
They just cannot see
Unshakeable spirit residing in me

It could have been easy
They gave me a chance
To become a puppet, and learn how to dance

I will not dance
I will not break
I will not sell out. I am not a fake

Remaining undaunted
I won't run and hide
I'll take my position here on the outside

Embracing my burden
My future is set
I have overcome though they don't see it yet

My struggle has ended
My anguish has ceased
I'll live out my days in relative peace

- Professor 929

27

Hate

Hate is a force
Snapping one's will
Hate is an agent with a license to kill

Hate is a lens
Which makes wrong seem right
Hate is a blinder, which robs us of sight

Hate is a beast
Devouring souls
Hate is a frost turning hearts cold

Hate is a seed
Planted by fears
Fed by abuse and watered with tears

Flame of destruction
Turning friend against friend
A tool of the wicked... the gravest of sin

Hate can be vanquished
Love is the key
Love is the lens that helps all to see

Love has the insight
To open up minds
Love has the power to break loose the binds

Love is compassion
To melt away fear
Love is the way to make hate disappear

- Professor 929

Warrior

"Stealth is my creed
And it's carefully planned
I move like the wind
As I creep through the land"

Vanguard

I am the vanguard
I do not know fear
Send me in first
I'm the tip of the spear

When others retreat
I always advance
When others decline
I jump at the chance

Don't worry about me
I will always survive
I'll complete the objective
And come out alive

Stealth is my creed
And it's carefully planned
I move like the wind
As I creep through the land

Soon after insertion
I cannot be found
I'm the invisible phantom
Lost in the background

I finish the mission
I do not leave a trace
I cover my tracks
As I head back to base

I need no reward
For the job that I've done
No medals required
I am just having fun

I am here when you need me
The consummate pro
Just give me a call
I am ready to go

- Professor 929

Phantom

They call me the Phantom
I live under cloak
I move undetected, just shadows and smoke

Fading to black
Just like a magician
Intangible ghost a mere apparition

I lie in the shadows
I stay out of view
Unseen and undaunted, I'm right next to you

Mysterious specter
An agent for good
I dwell in darkness I'm misunderstood

I counter act evil
I rest in their midst
I cannot be touched, I do not exist

Smooth and efficient
I glide as I flow
Beguiling, upsetting, eluding my foe

Sadly outmatched
They sweat and they cough
I'm shaken em, baking em, breaking em off

Apparently cornered
I've been here before
I leave them incensed as I vanish once more

Obsessed and dejected
As l remain free
I'm just an illusion. They'll never catch me

Professor 929

The Outer Edge

I have come to be a permanent resident of the Outer Edge

In solitude I dwell in danger.
On thin ice I do tread.

I choose to live where few dare to venture.
I choose to rest where men struggle to survive.

Pain is my mentor.
Adversity is my ally.

On the edge I have learned to prosper,
For the edge has made me grow.

It has come to be a proving ground for character,
Yet a fortress from vanity.

It has prepared me for tomorrow, come what may.

The edge is my home, and my dear old friend.

- Professor 929

Obsidian

Here on the scene
For a minute or two
I won't be here long, for I'm just passing through

Never at rest
At ease or at play
I stay about business no matter the day

Wars to be waged
And debts to be paid
The cards that I hold must be carefully played

Wrought by fire
Black as the night
Sharp as a blade and trained for the fight

Time holds no sway
It brings me no strife
For I serve the giver and the taker of life

So what is death?
Should I be afraid?
The wages of sin demand to be paid!

I shall not retreat
Nor flinch at the pain
Embracing my fate, I shall not complain

The moment has passed
So I'm moving on
One moment I'm here, the next I'll be gone

So, remember my name
As I pass through the door
Obsidian, the aged man of war

- Professor 929

Advocate

I am your advocate
Always here right on cue
You need someone who's looking out just for you

Walking down the path of life
I am right by your side
Watching your step, I'm your invisible guide

Your silent partner
You won't know when I'm there
In fact, it is best that you remain unaware

I'll stay out of view
While arranging things
I'm in the background yet I'm pulling strings

No need to thank me
I don't want you know
I do what I do 'cause' I want you to grow

Just focus on living
Please live for today
Stay true to yourself and I'll keep harm away

I'll stay by your side
I will fit like a glove
Protecting your life is a job that I love

I'll stay in the shadows
To protect you from bad
I will be the best friend that you ever had

- Professor 929

Samurai Sword

I am vigilant
Cognizant of the day
My mind does not wander. My vision won't stray

I protect the good
From evil each day
I will show no quarter to the dragons I slay

I am incomplete
Without my old friend
In the heat of the fight on him I depend

My friend is a blade
Eveready to deal
He sparkles, although he is high carbon steel

He's precisely balanced
And as strait as a laser
Crafted with skill and as sharp as a razor

My friend has been forged
In the furnace of truth
We came to be friends when I was but a youth

My friend is unique
I am glad he is mine
I carry him with me all of the time

Brothers for life
He's dear to my heart
My friend is truly a fine work of art

We've wandered the Earth
For eons of time
Meting out justice and punishing crime

At the end of each day
Peace is my reward
So, I stay on the watch with my Samurai Sword

- Professor 929

Warrior

In silence I move through the thickness of the night.
In solitude I stay perched between paradise and oblivion.
Ever vigilant, I stand to protect the righteous and the meek.

With a steady hand and steely eye I peer into the face of the dragon.
With a righteous shield and a mighty blade I fight for the Master's Glory.
Only He can sustain me now!

I am wounded, but still fighting.
I have been down, but never out.
I do my Master's bidding no matter the cost or pain.
Only He can heal me now!

Oh mighty sovereign, I am Your warrior. I will fight for your name sake until the very end.
Send me into the fray that I may offer a reply to your enemy.
Only You can deliver me now!

- Professor 929

Shadows

(US Special Forces)

I'm in an eight-man squad
And we're about to roll out
Another midnight run
Real danger no doubt

We got a secret mission
Humping gear twenty clicks
Keep it on the down low
Let's stay out of the mix

We'll stay in the bush
Travel way off the road
Gear up and move out
Let's lock and load

A surgical blade
We slice through the night
Deep in the jungle
Way out of sight

Shadows of the night
We creep through as they sleep
That's our MO
Run silent, run deep

Run up on some tangos
They aren't even aware
So we slide right on through
Then get into thin air

We pull a Houdini
For the rest of the night
No blood will be spilled
Before first morning light

We reach the objective
Before we see sun
Completely unnoticed
Another job well done

Hoo Ahh!

- Professor 929

Unit

My Unit is tight
Please make no mistake
We share a close bond
That nothing can break

When we're called for the fight
We appear with a quickness
Like a thief in the night
We creep in with a slickness

Like the fog off the bay
We roll in with a thickness
When we're deep in the fray
We get ill with a sickness

My crew moves as one
For we have but one sight
We float silently
Through the darkness of night

We are undefeated
A statement of fact
We roll in and bounce out
We're always in tact

If you see us coming
Your cover is blown
Don't make a mistake
Just leave it alone

We appear suddenly
In the blink of an eye
We take care of business
And then it's goodbye

This world is polluted
It's sad but it's true
But we take out the trash
That's just what we do

Professor 929

Point

I drew point
Now I'm all in the mix
With my head in the game and the squad on my six

It's a hazardous job
That I'm honored to do
I stay far ahead keeping heat off my crew

At one with the land
I track like a hound
I blaze a sure path but I don't make a sound

I remember the moment
The Sarge looked my way
He gave me the look there was nothing to say

I came for the fight
Now I'm ready to dance
But the Sergeant said,' Easy son, you'll get your chance'

'But I'll tell you right now
It just wouldn't be wise
We have to stay ghost 'cause' these hills have sharp eyes'

With the wisdom of ages
Etched deep in his face
The Sarge would get all of us out of this place

So now I'm all stealthy
I'm there in the clutch
Like Eliot Ness, I cannot be touched

With me at the point
We're in great shape
We'll stay out of sight as we make our escape

- Professor 929

The Cell

Last night I got the call
About a terrorist cell
From an inside source
A great piece of intel!

So I briefed all my men
As we grabbed all our gear
Then I looked in their faces
There were no signs of fear

We piled into the trucks
Then we rolled down the street
It's the usual plan
Gonna bring extreme heat

I didn't take any chances
As we sealed off the street
We rolled up in there strong
At the front door eight deep

I gave the signal to breach
As we took out the door
I sent in my point men
Then I sent in two more

Cleared the first couple rooms
The tension really increased
We need to be very thorough
While we're searching this piece

Then we rolled right up on them
They were really surprised
These guys were real frightened
Had that look in their eyes

My point man said FREEZE!
But they started to move
Don't know what they were thinking
So we took them down smooth

Took them out to the street
Put them all in the vans
We kept them alive
Though they had other plans

It was clear from the evidence
We just got there in time
They were making some bombs
We found maps of the crime

The papers we seized
Led us to the head clown
Now he's out of commission
'Cause we shut this cell down

- Professor 929

Buck Wild Willy

Buck-Wild Willy
Was a hell of a guy
He was mortally wounded but refused to die

My man Bill
Had notorious style
He had but two gears, laid back and buck-wild

Six foot four
Two eighty or so
He was always down and ready to go

Thunderous voice
Dark brown skin
Fearless and wise a leader of men

Down for the cause
He was ready to ride
No need for a care with Bill by your side

A valiant soldier
With plenty of soul
I'll ride with Buck Wild cause he's ready to roll

-Professor 929

Step Away From the Light

It's been a good while
Since you've fallen asleep
You make not a sound, you have fallen deep

Your outlook was grave
So we were surprised
When the surgical team said you were stabilized

They pieced you together
With sutures and glue
It's truly amazing what surgeons can do!

Now you are resting
Like nothing was wrong
I know you will rise because you are strong

You have a few scars
But they are minute
Your body has healed its time to reboot

I will not lose hope
I will not despair
It is time to rely on the power of prayer

We will not give up
By now you should know
I promise you brother we won't let you go

Come back to us brother
Please open your eyes
This is not the time for tearful goodbyes

This is not your time
This is not your end
Step away from the light, it is not your friend!

- Professor 929

Awakening

I'd sustained heavy damage
And the pain was surreal
So, I had to withdraw and take time to heal

I had no more strength
For my wounds were too deep
So, my body shut down as I fell fast asleep

I've been hibernating
For an awful long time
Though my visions of slumber were truly sublime

Much time had gone by
Seems I've been down for ages
It would seem that my brain was rebooting in stages

My vision now lucid
I wake from my rest
I plot my next moves, as my thoughts coalesce

I've been undercover
My wounds healed at length
My soul is repaired and abundant in strength

I've been well concealed
As I've remained withdrawn
I'll come out of hiding, the danger is gone

I'm eager to fight
And get back in the game
I'll return to my mission, my vision, my name

Repairs are complete
There is nothing I lack
I'm ready for battle. It is great to be back!

- Professor 929

Sacred Contract

We go off to war
Fighting side by side
Between us my brother there exist no divide

As we prepare for battle
We all make a pact
'Leave no one behind', that's our sacred contract!

For you I will go
To hell and beyond
I won't leave you behind, my word is my bond

We've won many battles
As we fought back to back
Then one night our foe launched a well-planned attack

We were over run
We had to retreat
We barely survived as I tasted defeat

I called out your name
And heard not a sound
We scoured the land but you could not be found

When the chaos ensued
They took you away
We were ordered to base but we opted to stay

We'll not leave without you
We made up a plan
We 'd launch our offensive and retrieve our man

We went in with no fear
As we took back the hill
They had to retreat as we shattered their will

The thought of your anguish
Made my soul burn
Now our foe we have vanquished and we have returned

- Professor 929

Blood on My Hands

We launched from the ship
By the cover of night
The moon was not full so we stayed out of sight

We disembarked
Then crept up the shore
It just comes easy. We've done this before

I've not come in peace
I'm here to wage war
I am on your land. I'm at your front door

But something is different
No fire inside
No thoughts of bravado or national pride

The reasons we're here
Were apparently fake
You simply have something that we plan to take

This mission is wrong
I clearly see
To tell you the truth this just isn't me

I became a soldier
To battle oppression
Now I'm being misused for an evil obsession

Compromised leaders
Have lost their way
It's clear that I can't trust a word that they say

I have seen things
Which are hard to face
I have done things that I cannot erase

My conscience is tortured
Despite the abuse
Just following orders is not an excuse

As I reflect deep
It's tougher to sleep
Despite what I've done I know life isn't cheap

So, I've had enough
You must understand
I won't have more innocent blood on my hands

- Professor 929

The Way of the Sword

Alone with my thoughts
My soul is at rest
Feeling my heart at work in my chest

Perched on a hill
Where nothing remains
Beyond the trees, on the wind-swept planes

A desolate wasteland
Barren and cold
Lay the sun bleached bones of the soldiers of old

Absorbed for a time
With barely a sound
I ponder before me the blood soaked ground

The swords of the past
Devoted to rust
Their masters have passed and returned to the dust

Resting in tombs
With nothing to say
The memory of legends has faded away

They lived by the sword
They fought, then they fell
Alone and asleep and residing in hell

The warrior's craft
Was once understood
The business was death, and business was good

Rotting corpses
Littered the ground
Buzzards feasting on flesh by the pound

But, man has learned
A better way
Ushering forth a promising day

Leaving behind
The weapons of wrath
Walking upon a spiritual path

People working
Hand in hand
Peace has settled upon the land

Love has flooded the world
At last!
Washing away the sins of the past

Freedom reigns
Upon this day
The former things have passed away

No crusades
For golden rings
They do not seek the crown of the kings

No more hunting
With arrows of flame
No more killing for fortune or fame

An end
To the wailing warrior's cry
An end to the sorrow of bidding goodbye

A moment of time
To sing to the young
Singing the songs that need to be sung

Taking delight
In the craft of the hand
Enjoying the bountiful fruit of the land

Feeding the hungry
And clothing the poor
An end to the deafening sonnets of war

Babies are born
Rejoicing at birth
Men and women are filling the earth

An end to the hatred
Budding from fear
Deleting the reason for sorrow and tear

Children spared
From paying the cost
Avoiding the pain of innocence lost

Conquering
The broken sword
Peace is now the hearts reward

-Professor 929

Zero

Zero is the sum
Of the empty hand
Zero is a dessert in a desolate land

Zero is the product
Of a starving mind
Naught will be spared who choose to stay blind

Violence is a failure...
Which threatens all life
Zero are the blessings at the end of a knife

Peace is the product
Of the open door
Zero is the outcome from the evils of war

Wealth is pursued
In numerous ways
Zero is the balance at the end of the days

Zero is the wage
In death I will earn
From dust I was made. To dust I return.

- Professor 929

Sentiments

"No matter the depths
Of the pit of the night
Keep steadily marching on into the light

No matter how high
Or dreaded the wall
Never give up, although you may fall"

Hope

Hope is the power
That keeps me alive
Devoid of all hope, I could not survive

The beacon of light
That brightens my heart
Hope will keep me from coming apart

The sum of all goodness
Intangible dream
Hope is a river that starts as a steam

Hope is my refuge
When moments look bleak
Hope keeps me strong although I am weak

Hope is a gift
Preserving the soul
Hope will keep me from losing control

The forecast is dim
And filled with a dread
The days will be stormy and dark up ahead

Hope provides vision
My eyes remain free
The darker the road, the more I can see

No matter the peril
I will not fear
With hope in my heart, my path remains clear

Alone in the dark
At the end of my rope
I will persevere because I have hope

- Professor 929

Love
(1 Corinthians 13:4-7)

Love is a sculptor
Transforming a man
Love is a God with a merciful hand

Love begets love
It's quite plain to see
Unconditional love will come to you free

Love has the power
To re-wright the slate
Love has the power to conquer all hate

Love is the greatest
Power we seek
It has healed the wounded, the broken, the weak

Love is the greatest
Gift one can give
Love gives us the hope and a reason to live

Mother to child
Husband to wife
Love is a grand celebration of life

Absolute love
Will lessen the sting
It buffers the pain that living can bring

Tenderly cherished
And handled with care
Love is a treasure all people can share

It doesn't see bias
Nor color of skin
Love is the Way to wash away sin

The purest of love
Will always prevail
Remember my friend, love will never fail!

- Professor 929

Trials

Problems in bunches
Seem too much to manage
I try to survive while I mitigate damage

Exhausted and desperate
I struggle to cope
This mess is so stressful I start to lose hope

Then I remember
What Dad always said
Step back for a moment and then clear your head

Emotions unchecked
Are just a distraction
Panic and fear are improper reactions

Dissect the chaos
No time for self doubt
Keep a clear head and you'll figure it out

You must formulate
A suitable plan
Be sure to stay focused on the task at hand

Keep it together
You know what to do
Just work the problem. Don't let it work you!

- Professor 929

Heart

Your opponent is winning
You cannot hide
Huffing and puffing with nothing inside

He strikes you once more
A terrible blow
Your eyes start to dim, you start to let go

Your body goes limp
You fall to your knees
Your vision grows dim. Your brain starts to freeze

But you will not give up
As he stands over you
Then you notice your bleeding all over your shoe

Now you are livid
Back up on your feet
This round isn't over. This fight's not complete!

You reach down inside
Feeling renewed
Feeling like you just have nothing to loose

You strike your opponent again and again
You think to yourself
I am going to win!

Your rival now falters
He has fallen down
He yields to defeat as he rests on the ground

You've vanquished your foe
He's fallen apart
You have persevered because you have heart

- Professor 929

56

Never Give Up!

Imperfect man
Plagued with regret
Afflicted and tortured and saddled with debt

Don't give up
On the hope up ahead
No matter the pain or the words that are said

No matter the depths
Of the pit of the night
Keep steadily marching on into the light

No matter how high
Or dreaded the wall
Never give up, although you may fall

You cannot be beaten
Nor vanquished by sin
Remember your goal and never give in

I've been there with you
Each time that you've cried
Remember my friend; I'm right by your side

You may feel alone
With burden to bare
As if you had no one to love you, or care

It is an illusion
That just isn't true
Remember that people are counting on you

Without your love
They would stand alone
Lost and afraid and out on their own

Accepting defeat
Just wouldn't be right
So, never surrender. Don't give up the fight!

-Professor 929

Live

I enter a room
Alone and depressed
Tortured of spirit and wanting of rest

Broken and battered
I cannot go on
I'll only have peace the moment I'm gone

I sit in the corner
And let out a cry
Praying to live but wanting to die

Alone in the darkness
Barely alive
Just me, a bottle and my 45

Thought and emotion
A most toxic blend
I mull it all over for hours on end

My time is at hand
There's no room for doubt
Deciding to stay, or go and check out

The moment of truth
Is finally here
My mind is so clouded and crippled with fear

Images flashing
In my mind's eye
Memories are vividly passing me by

Recounting the moments
Of laughter and song
The things I did right and the things I did wrong

The people I love
The old and the youth
The joy and the pain, the lies and the truth

My loved ones would sorrow
Should I disappear
I could not protect them if I were not here

Clinging to life
By one tattered thread
My thoughts become ordered and clear in my head

I entered this room
Right on the brink
But this moment alone has caused me to think

I have obligations
That I haven't met
I must not give in and check out just yet

I have to help others
The meek and the bold
The broken of heart, the young and the old

I will carry on
Though I'm but a man
I'll have to make peace wherever I can

I feel reborn
I have a fresh start
With no doubts in my head and no fear in my heart

There's so little time
And so much to give
At the end of my stay I've chosen to live.

- Professor 929

Phoenix

I stand in the ruins
I taste my demise
I hear lamentation and desperate cries

The life that I built
Has now been destroyed
My blood, sweat and tears are now null and void

My years of hard work
Have all been in vain
I'm somewhat bewildered. This all seems insane!

I won't be defeated
I will not submit
I tell you my friend I will never quit!

In the midst of the chaos
Upheavals and clashes
A fiery phoenix, I rise from the ashes

I've nothing to loose
I've only to gain
I've endured much anguish, torment and pain

I must rebuild me
I stand at square one
My story's not over. I have just begun!

Life is a riddle
It will leave you confused
In order to gain sometimes you must lose

I will persevere
Yes! I will prevail
Believe what I say. I just will not fail!

- Professor 929

Liberation

Fighting:
An incredible waste of my time
I respect yours but you won't respect mine!

Understanding is critical
For you and for me
You close your eyes tight, so you won't have to see

Get your way all the time?
Why that hardly seems fair
Devoid of all logic, compassion or care

You are without reason,
What more can I do?
I'll get up, and get out, for I'm leaving you

An unfortunate circumstance
All will agree
This is a conclusion that just should not be

Changing my course
I have a new track
With promise ahead I shall not look back

Unburdened by misery
Freedom taste good
Living unfettered as human beings should

I am me again!
I don't have to hide
I laugh and I jump for I'm happy inside

I wish you the best
No grudges I bear
Happiness to you, and please do take care.

- Professor 929

Escape

Another day of pain
My world is filled with strife
It's like getting sliced apart with a rusty kitchen knife

I'm glad I'm at the end
I made it through this day
I'll crawl inside this bottle and then slowly fade away

I need to get a grip
And find a better way to cope
I must remember now that where there's life there's also hope

I think about escape
It's always on my mind
Trading my torment for a different hell of another kind

I think I'm going to leave
My state of mind is dire
I'll leave this frying pan and take a leap into the fire

I'm going to take that leap
I will not look twice
I think I have a chance. It's a roll of the dice

I have to be real cautious
And land up on my feet
To finally taste success will be a gift that is most sweet

My mind and heart are free
Now I can finally grow
I've been suppressed for ages I should have done this long ago

Now I've slipped my chains
I'll travel very far
Freedom will restore my heart and time will heal my scar

- Professor 929

Quest

I have lost my direction
'Cause' life's been a bit much
I forgot who I was for I fell out of touch

So, I'm off on a journey
While I am free
I will go on a quest. I have got to find me

I know there'll be trials
And tests up ahead
I will be alert as I watch where I tread

My future's uncertain
But that is alright
I'll not take too much for I'm traveling light

I'll break loose the chains
That kept me in the dark
I will walk this path with a wide open heart

I'll live in the moments
As they come my way
I will dwell in the minutes that belong to each day

My time is at hand
But first I will pray
I'll wait for first light, then I'll be on my way

As I see the sun rise
I gather my things
I soon will take flight though I do not have wings

Completely equipped
Refreshed and prepped
My journey begins with one miniscule step

As I start on my way
There is nothing I lack
With the wind in my hair, and the sun on my back

- Professor 929

Relax

Relax my friend
Things aren't quite that bad
To see you this way is terribly sad

All stressed out
And you do not know why
Often you look like you're going to cry

All wound up
Don't know what to do
Anxiety is just no good for you

Don't get me wrong
I do understand
At times things don't go according to plan

The clock's always ticking
It seems such a crime
Too much to do and not enough time

All of this weight
You need to unload
One more issue and you may explode

Ease up my friend
Take a deep breath
Or else you just might be worried to death

Dwell on the good
In spite of the bad
Ponder the blessings that have made you glad

Watch a sunset
A glorious sight
Ponder the stars in the heavens at night

Remember your friends
All the kind acts
Believe in tomorrow and try to relax

- Professor 929

Music

A song in my head
A beat in my heart
Deeply in love with the lyrical art

Check my flow
As I bounce down the street
Completely immersed in an intricate beat

Infused with a rhythm
Down deep in my soul
Right on the edge but still in control

My inner most being
In sync with the time
I have become one with the rhythm and rhyme

I blissfully linger
Upon every note
I live in the words that the song writer wrote

Lifted up
As though I had wings
The Diva is free in the song that she sings

Tenderly held
In a song that embraces
I'm venturing off to melodious places

Absorbed in a realm
Saturated by sound
I'm lost and I'm free and I cannot be found

Floating about
And feeling no pain
Euphonious fingers messaging my brain

My eyes are closed
Though I am not blind
Audio vistas are blowing my mind

Invigorated
Floating on air
Sliding through space with hardly a care

Faithfully guided
By pure melody
It's Quadraphonic navigation. You see?

Snapping my fingers
And moving my toes
I follow the music where ever it goes

Here on my own
Enjoying this tone
Soothing my soul, right down to the bone

A heavenly gift
That keeps me believing
Music; the gift I keep on receiving

-Professor 929

Deep Blue Sea

Immersed in a world
Without window or wall
Just floating about with no cares at all

I'm so overwhelmed
I'm in disbelief
All the species and colors that make up this reef

I'm surrounded by beauty
I just have to smile
As my bottle nosed friends play with me for a while

Weightless and floating
Can't stay in one place
I'm drifting about like I'm in outer space

I really love diving
I've got to be me
I should be at work but I've got to be free

All the wealth in the world
Doesn't mater to me
I prefer to reside in the deep blue sea

- Professor 929

The Park

A stroll in the park
On a warm summer day
Trees line the path, to show me the way

The cool summer breeze
Refreshes my soul
Walking is healthy, so I've been told

The sun on my shoulders
Feels good to my bones
I take off my shoes and walk on the stones

I've come to a clearing
At the edge of the lake
I see a boat pass, and then I study its wake

It comes to the shore
And covers my toes
The smell of fresh water tickles my nose

The sounds of the summer
They do make me smile
So I'll sit on this rock, and stay for a while

An out of doors symphony
Is there for the asking
I hear bird conversation, and young children laughing

A bee flying by
A cowbell rings
I hear a humming bird beating its wings

It's getting late
But I won't leave just yet
I'll sit by the lake, and watch the sun set

- Professor 929

Woods

Alone in the woods
I rest as I sit
Taking time out from my canoe trip

The ground is alive
With an emerald hew
All speckled with sunlight and patches of dew

The trees are fantastic
Enormously tall
They don't loose their leaves in the middle of fall

It's peaceful and silent
I let out a sigh
I notice a baby deer wandering by

Some squirrels are playing
Frolicking free
A red and black butterfly lands on my knee

Such a heavenly banquet
A real treat to behold
Nature provides a grand feast for my soul

- Professor 929

Garden

I'm planting a garden
With Mom and with Dad
Working the earth makes me feel glad

I'm off to the garden
With the seeds that I'll sow
It's truly a privilege making plants grow

I'll plant some tomatoes
Right there in a line
I'll mark off this section with red and white twine

We'll plant us some corn
Right over here
I have to call dibs on the very first ear

Moms planting potatoes
In a very small patch
I know they'll be tasty just like the last batch

Dad's planting melons
Way back in the rear
I hope there're enormous just like last year

When we're all done
We'll sit in the shade
And look at the beautiful garden we made

- Professor 929

Spaghetti Carbonara

It's a beautiful day
And it's great how I feel
So I'll take some time out to plan a good meal

I'll go to South Philly
To get all my food
The sights and the sounds put me in the right mood

I park the car
And pick up some meat
Then I head up the block and turn right on 9th Street

I pick up some veggies
Form my favorite place
The owner is cool and has really great taste

Now I'll pick up some cheese
My trip's almost complete
My last stop is DiBruno's 930, 9th Street

I get back to my house
It's great to be home
I'll get right down to business now that I am alone

I put on some water,
Bring it to a boil,
Use a pound of pancetta and wrap the rest in foil

I cook it all up
And step out back to eat
Ah! A meal in my garden is always a treat

Spaghetti Carbonara
And a smooth Chardonnay
What a fine way to enjoy a cool autumn day

- Professor 929

Friday

Friday at last
Another week for the book
I head out for home without a second look

I hop in my ride
And head down the road
I switch my brain onto the weekend mode

I pull up to my place
As my heart starts to soar
A twist of the key, then I'm in the front door

I draw a hot bath
Put on Sade
Ease back with a Scotch and reflect on the day

I've touched so many people
In so many ways
In so many venues on so many days

I enjoy people
They're really worthwhile
I like conversation and making them smile

I throw on my clothes
And check out my hair
I'm off to see friends at a lively affair

The people are happy
The music is loud
I wade into the people and fade into the crowd

I'm up in the zone
I'm feeling all right
I'm free and easy on a live Friday night.

- Professor 929

Welcome

Welcome my friend
I am so glad that you came
In the room at the rear we are watching the game

Please come right this way
I have saved you a chair
Help yourself to some snacks they are right over there

If you need to wash up
Over there is a sink
Feel free to mingle while I pour you a drink

Would you like collard greens?
And a flame broiled steak?
After dinner we're having some Black Forest cake

Here is your drink
And your plate piled with food
I hope that this meal puts you in a good mood

If you get tired of sitting
Please feel free to roam
Remember my friend; my house is your home

Oh did I mention
There's a group playing cards
They are in the gazebo right in the backyard

Sometime after four
The DJ will arrive
The friends will be dancing. It's bound to get live

Have a good time
Get lost in the crowd
Feel free to let loose, and feel free to get loud

- Professor 929

A Dream

I have a dream
I need to help others
I'll bring some relief to my sisters and brothers

I am here to serve
I'm not here to judge
If you need motivating I'll give you a nudge

If you're dieing of thirst
I will bring you a drink
If you're right on the edge I'll pull you from the brink

If you're out in the cold
I'll bring you some heat
And while I am there I'll bring shoes for your feet

If you're out on the street
And you don't have a bed
I will help build a roof over your head

If you can't find your way
And your vision is blurred
You just need some hope I will bring you the Word

Our Father above
Knows just what we need
He gives us the knowledge we need to succeed

I've been down and out
With nothing to lose
Believe me my friend I've walked in your shoes

Do not give up hope
Don't give in to doubt
I am living proof that there is a way out

So keep your head up
Someday this will pass
You'll see that this struggle is not going to last

Someday you will make it
I know you'll succeed
Then you can help others who are still in need

Teach

Blessed are the ones
Who reach the unreachable
Possessing the gift to teach the unteachable

With open hearts
They nurture the mind
Teachers are mighty, patient and kind

Forging the road
For posterity
What nobler cause could there ever be?

Imparting knowledge
Wisdom and truth
Refining the hearts and minds of the youth

Illiterate souls
Taught how to read
The timid of spirit trained how to lead

The selfish of heart
Encouraged to share
The indifferent stone inspired to care

Compassionate words
Carefully spoken
Healing the spirit that has become broken

Fearlessly rescuing
Those who are sinking
Saving the ones who act without thinking

Fondly remembered
By those you have reached
How could they learn without someone to teach?

- Professor 929

Mom

What can I say?
You already know
You brought me forth; then helped me grow

You nourished my body
And nurtured my mind
You've always been loving, patient and kind

You showed me the Way
And built my insight
You skillfully taught me the wrong from the right

You guided my path
With rarely a shout
And when I stepped wrong you straitened me out

Never a doubt
That you always care
Your love is honest, courageous and fair

You've proven unbreakable
Down through the years
You've suffered much heartache and shedding of tears

Your path was not easy
But clearly I see
No matter the test you were there for me

Your love is profound
I often reflect
I'll always love you with the greatest respect

I honor you now
With this humble rhyme
You'll be in my heart till the end of my time

- Professor 929

Dad

You lived to the full
And now you are gone
Though your moments in memories are bound to live on

In the hearts and the minds
Of the souls that you touched
The times spent with you we all treasure so much

Just looking around
At the friends that you made
Your smile, and your words, and your deeds shall not fade

Please know that we miss you
Things aren't quite the same
I don't live a day without speaking your name

Recalling the times
We would go for a walk
Enjoying the journey as we took time to talk

We talked about life
And the lessons we've learned
We pondered the depth of the knowledge we earned

We dreamed of the future
And studied the past
It seemed that your time has passed by much too fast

I miss you dear father
I wish I cry
I often remember that spark in your eye

What I wouldn't give
For more time with you
But the time that we shared will carry me through

I will not despair
My kindhearted friend
For I know in my heart that I'll see you again

- Professor 929

Pop Pop
(1934-2009)

This is a troubled time
Our dear loved one we have lost
It saddens all our hearts that he's paid the highest cost

His soul will be remembered
By our Father up above
He touches all our hearts as we think of him with love

No doubt that we will miss him
In the days that are ahead
As we mourn our beloved brother, many tears will be shed

But let's step back for a moment
Reminiscing for a while
Let's think about the way he used to make us laugh and smile

Remember how he wore...
His favorite hat upon his head?
Remember all the funny things that Pop Pop often said?

He loved messing with the kids
But never made them cry
Remember how he always had that sparkle in his eye?

But if you think about it
This is not quite the end
Let's dream about the day we'll be together with our friend

- Professor 929

My Little Girls

Raising my daughters
Has made me whole
They have become quite the sight to behold

Beautiful hearts
With dazzling smiles
When they go out places they do it in style

Ladies no doubt
But tomboys with me
It's hard to keep up as their spirits run free

When my girls speak
Focus I must : -)
Speaking at warp speed leaves me in the dust

My greatest gifts
I'll say it out loud
These two little women have made me real proud!

For you I have love
Know this to be true
I will always be there for the two of you

As I see you grow older
I silently sigh
Someday when you grow up and leave I will cry

Brilliantly glowing
Like the finest of pearls
You'll never stop being my little girls

- Professor 929

Sunshine

Sunshine I love you
Inducing a smile
With your cheery outlook and positive style

Eloquent spirit
Quite the delight
Your words are so thoughtful, kindhearted and bright

This world is unkind
And terribly bad
At times it makes my heart horribly sad

Your garrulous charm
Is a fine art
Walking with Sunshine repairs my heart

Benevolent daughter
Perennial light
Your kindness can brighten the darkest of night

I'm anxious to see you
Just like the dawn
I'm glad when you're near and sad when you're gone

If you were not you
This world would seem strange
I pray that your attitude will never change

You may be petite
Though in spirit you're tall
Never bitter of soul or petty or small

Grateful my daughter
That you are mine
A treasure so pure, you are my Sunshine

- Professor 929

Siani the Brave

Siani the Brave
With the warrior's heart
I am always with you although we're apart

I am proud of you
So wise yet so young
Your name's always right on the tip of my tongue

I speak of you often
To the people I meet
I tell them you're strong and yet you are sweet

I think of you much
I'll bet every hour
I see your smile bloom like a beautiful flower

I hear your voice laugh
And singing a song
I think of you well, I think of you long

Charming and honest
I just love your style
We must get together and chat for a while

We must make the time
Just you and me
Perhaps we can talk over cookies and tea

I am thinking of you
Stay well and live smart
Remember I love you with all of my heart

-Professor 929

My Boy

You're the ying to my yang
Pull me up when I'm down
I've got your back covered all the way across town

Got love for your people
They're my people too
Your folks are my folks we're all in the same crew

In for a Benjamin
In for a pound
I'll roll with you brother. I'm down if you're down

No one will defeat you
While I'm standing by
I'll fight by your side, for you I would die

Can't separate us
You can try if you please
Cause my brother and I are as thick as thieves

To see your success
Brings me great joy
You're a hell of a man, but you're always my boy!

- Professor 929

Little Sister

Hey little sister
Tell me what's new?
You look kind of down.
What's troubling you?

Come lean on my shoulder
And talk for while
All silent and saddened
It's just not your style

Please pour out your heart
Whisper or shout
It's just you and me
So, let it all out

Is it a guy?
Who's broken your heart?
Tell me his name
I'll rip him apart!

Don't be ashamed
So what if you cry
You'll start to feel better
As time passes by

Come hold my hand
Let loose your tears
I'm all finished speaking
In fact, I'm all ears

- Professor 929

Friend

Life is the mountain
We all have to climb
It can make us both weaker and stronger with time

At times this world
Is a treacherous place
Alone it's a challenge that no one should face

Despite all the challenges
We remain tight
Our bond has survived the darkest of night

We carry each other
A fact that is true
You've been there for me; I'll be there for you

We've managed to build
A trust that's unshakeable
Our friendship has proven to be most unbreakable

I'll be by your side
Right down to the end
I'm blessed to have such a wonderful friend!

- Professor 929

Commentary

"Immersed in the fury
Of those you disrespect
What you'll feel upon you is the trickle down
effect"

The Bean Counter

The age of reason is over. The day of the Bean Counter is here!

Bean $ Counter (bĕnn koun'tər), ɳ. **1.** A member of a growing religious order worshiping money, devoid of vision, morals or common sense. Working counter to the benefit of the common good. **2.** adj. *slang*. Meant as an insult for someone lacking compassion, vision or intestinal fortitude – greedy gutless worm. **3.** adj. A master in the art of deception. A worker of hyperbole. An expert in number crunching (*manipulation*)

The Bean Counter (*Stupidicus-Rex*) has been known to put profits ahead of the needs of his fellow man and society in general. The Bean Counter can be identified by his single-breasted blue or gray suit, his poorly styled comb over and his inability to see past the next quarterly dividend. Evidence of the Bean Counter's handiwork can be seen in the sharp rise of homelessness and unemployment, global warming, international terrorism, the destruction of the global economy and a meltdown in Western industrial innovation. The stench of decay, mediocrity and greed follow him in all his endeavors. He is the harbinger of death, and anything he touches is doomed.

The Bean Counter's natural habitats are the boardrooms of corporate America. He is also known to inhabit some political offices. Wall Street is a favored spawning ground of the Bean Counter. A nocturnal creature; it usually prefers to do its' handiwork in the dark, away from the prying eyes of regulators, advocacy groups and the general public. It has been known to eat its' own young and sell its' grandparents for a mere promise of a percentage. Approach with extreme caution as its' bite is extremely toxic and quite contagious. If you find yourself cornered by one of these nefarious creatures speak to it in truthful, logical sentences so as to confuse it. Then make your escape. The Bean Counter has been known to recoil at the sight of an investigative reporter wielding a camera and/ or microphone.

If you see a Bean Counter infiltrating your organization and slowly seizing control you must contain and neutralize him with extreme urgency. Finally, he must be surgically removed and disposed of like the malignant tumor he is. Failure to do so will result in your organization's demise due to the erosion of innovation, talent and ethics.

This has been a public service announcement from Professor 929. Stay tuned… more to follow.

- P929

The Suit

It was a family owned business
Back in the day
Superior benefits, excellent pay

The owner had vision
Just look where he's been
He took care of us, we took care of him

But the owner got older, and passed the baton
Enter the sons
The good times were gone

They did not like working
It made us all mad
Apparently they were nothing like Dad

Behind the closed doors they started to say
Why should we work?
When we could go play

Working is really a sucker's game
We have all Dad's money, his fortune, his fame

Indifferent to workers
Quick to raise doubt
Secretly plotting to go and cash out

So they brought in the suit;
Bean counter by trade
Had no knowledge of the products we made

Made us bid on the jobs
We've been doing for years
He treated us poorly, and managed with fear

Remember when managers valued our work?
Then the suite arrived
Man, what a jerk!

Then later that year
The sons were real pleased
The suit took our company way over seas

The suit was a fraud, a phony, a fake
We heard as he shouted
'Let them eat cake!'

- Professor 929

Empty Houses

Empty houses all in a row
Where are the people?
Where did they go?

Packed up and slipped out
By the cover of night
No dignity left, no hope, no fight

Their jobs disappeared
Through no fault of their own
And as a result they are leaving their home

The family is homeless
But the bank does not care
Leaving this family in utter despair

Where will they go?
Where will they sleep?
They must join the ranks of the ones on the street

The women and children
They too have to go
To live in the harshness, the heat and the snow

Politicians don't care
It's really quite grim
Unwilling to help, it can't happen to them

Death roams the streets
Just like the grim reaper
Do we really believe we're our brother's keeper?

Now the house still sits empty
So I've been told
Yet this family remains out in the cold

Steps must be taken
To stop this vile sin
The question is now, Where to begin?

- Professor 929

Homeless

Unfortunate soul
I just don't see why
When winter comes, our poor brother should die

Frozen and lifeless
Naked and bare
People step over him like he's not there

They think to themselves
Hearts callused and tough
That fellow just did not work quite hard enough

Is this the society?
In which we now live?
Where it's greater to take and it's foolish to give

That logic seems backward
Short sighted and vile
Suppose you lived out on the street for a while?

You don't think it's possible?
Can't happen to you?
It can happen to anyone, believe me it's true

We must not accept it
Foreclosures are evil
The process produces yet more homeless people

We must stop this madness
We should all assist
We've got to do better; we're better than this!

- Professor 929

Hunger

Hunger's a phantom
Gorging on prey
Children are starving and dying today

Nations lay silent
With nothing to say
Surely we can't believe this is Ok?

Thousands will pass
Before the next day
Starvation's a price that infants now pay

Defenseless and fragile
Unable to feed
They truly epitomize humans in need

Born into hunger
Their hearts are depressed
Beginning their lives completely oppressed

Sowing the seeds
Of injustice and strife
Are we really okay with disposable life?

No hope for the famished
No options to choose
Spawning whole regions with nothing to loose

Rulers are playing
A dangerous game
Taking advantage and passing the blame

So, no help will arrive
From far away lands
The children now fade in the heat of the sands

- Professor 929

Hey Mister

Hey Mister
Can you please spare a dime?
I'm hungry, I'm tired, and I haven't much time.

I need your help
To be perfectly clear
I cannot survive. I'm dying out here!

It's hard to sleep
There's no bed for me
Constantly moving, I'm homeless you see

Police came one day
And then made us leave
They threw out our things. It's hard to believe.

My brother and sister
My Mom and my Dad
We lost everything that we ever had

My parents had jobs
That went overseas
No money put us in a pretty tight squeeze

We went to the bank
In search of a loan
But we were denied. So they shut off our phone

They finally came
In the middle of night
They shut off the water, the heat and the lights

Eviction came next
So, now here we are
Living together in one little car

I still go to school
But I struggle to learn
My stomach makes noises and constantly burns

So I'm asking you please
As I travel this street
I cannot survive without something to eat!

-Professor 929

Give and Take

It takes all kinds of people
To make the world go around
Some people lift us and some bring us down

You've got people who give
And people who take
Some keeping it real and some who are fake

A giver is a person
Who knows how to live
He tries to help others with the power to give

A taker is concerned
With taking your wealth
He brings blight on mankind only thinking of self

A giver is a person
Spreading good there's no doubt
A taker is a clown we can all do without

If everyone gave
We would all have much more
If everyone took we would all be at war

Unjustly hurting
And killing each other
Greedily robbing our sister and brother

Selfishly grabbing
It does not make sense
Getting our way at our neighbor's expense

It has all been written
At James Chapter Four
Open the Word if you want to know more.

The giver or taker
What's your point of view?
The question at hand is which one are you?

- Professor 929

Unsustainable

We live in an age
That is unexplainable
We live in a way that is quite unsustainable

How did this happen?
What are we thinking?
Our resources seem to be steadily shrinking

We consume
More than we produce
This is a disgrace! There is no excuse!

The world that we built
Is in its demise
Gone are the thinkers, the brave and the wise

The builders, the dreamers
The strong and the bold
The mighty of spirit, the legends of old

The age of reason
Has faded away
We've mortgaged tomorrow to live for today

Crumbling roads
Mortar and bricks
We do not possess the money to fix

Governing structures
Completely unwound
Our cities are tumbling right to the ground

Checkmate my friends
We have fallen prey
Our skies are now filled with the stench of decay

Greed is the path
We decided to take
We were arrogant. We made a mistake

History teaches
Though we never learn
Rome had to fall. I guess it's our turn!

Professor 929

Bistro

Welcome to the Bistro
Come in and meet the crew
I am known as "The Suit"
I will be serving you

No need of reservations
Just come in and sit down
There's always room for many more
On the shady side of town

Come and taste the poverty
A bitter meal to eat
Simmered with a misery
So sparse and incomplete

Drink the wine of insolence
Hand crafted by a few
Created for the masses
A cold and bitter brew

Serving up our specialty
It is our sacred wish
We plan to feed the world
Our most prolific dish

A stew of apathetic lies
Roasted to perfection
Seasoned with the salt of greed
Devoid of all affection

For dessert may I suggest?
The soufflé of deceit
A masterpiece of treachery
Delicious, light and sweet

The Bistro of oppression
A virtual Gourmet
The meals have been prepared with care
Please do enjoy your stay

- Professor 929

Owed to the Suit

To all the suits out there
I have some words for you
Your fate has now been sealed
By the wicked that you do

You cheated all your brothers
As you perpetrated wrong
But your days have now been numbered
Your time is almost gone

You tally up your profits
While your victims sob and weep
But the evil that you've sown
Soon you are going to reap

You pushed it way too far
You just don't understand
You got a tad too greedy
You over played your hand

You had to have it all
You could have spread the wealth
Making all these enemies
Is not good for your health

You've made yourself a target
What an unwise thing to do
We'll formulate a plan
Then we'll come looking for you

We'll take back what you've stolen
Together we will stand
You robbed us of our futures
Now we'll pry yours from your hand

Then you will have nothing
It did not have to be
You brought this on yourself
Because you would not see

Know that it has been written
Soon it will come to pass
The last shall be the first
And the first shall be the last

- Professor 929

Ethical Way

Ethics and the bottom line
Both can be elusive
But they are by no means mutually exclusive

Why not pursue both?
Think high proficiency
You can have it all; it's high efficiency

Commerce and life
They are intertwined
We've been making transactions since the dawn of mankind

Business is not difficult
Just do what is right
Don't lay down with dogs someday they will bite

It's just common sense
No need for degrees
Be leery of those who tout their expertise

Never forget
Why you started this trip
Don't let the Bean Counter take over your ship

Remain humble and true
Don't get caught in the game
Always take the high road, and stay free of blame

Be fair to all people
Make them your concern
Send them away happy and they'll always return

Do not be ensnared
With the schemes of the day
Always do things in an ethical way

-   Professor 929

More

I must subdue
All of creation
It's part of my plan for world domination

My fraud is an art
Your blindness is chronic
Flawless planned yet somewhat ironic

John Q. you're so easy
You just do not think
I'll make more cool aid and laugh as you drink.

The odds that you'll see
Are very remote
I will keep you at one another's throat

While you're fighting each other
And creating strife
I'm quietly seizing control of your life

I'll keep you distracted
So you cannot see
It's not about you. It's all about me!

I'm taking it all
Who's keeping score?
I don't have enough. I must have more!

I'll use you all up
Then show you the door
You will have nothing. Then I will have more!

Devoid of all morals
I profit from war
I'll sacrifice you so that I may have more!

The love of all money
And wealth I adore
I must have it all. I've got to have more!

Professor 929

101

Time to Pay the Piper

Time to pay the Piper
We new this day would come
Relentless and on tempo like the pounding of a drum

You knew what you were doing
You chose the short term gain
Now it would appear that we're in for long term pain

You gambled with the futures
Of those you have not met
Your actions have just voided all their toil, plans and sweat

Cavalier and arrogant
Proclaiming greed is right
Debased in all your values, myopic is your sight

You worship gold and silver
Your gods are incomplete
When they've lost their value they'll be thrown into the street

When your world has crumbled
Then what will you do?
Your golden god of greed shall not arrive to rescue you

Immersed in the fury
Of those you disrespect
What you'll feel upon you is the trickle down effect

Yesterday's aristocrat
Sheltered and exempt
Now it seems that you are held in unrepressed contempt

Hanging by a thread
You're running out of road
The world you built upon a lie is ready to implode

Judgment has been rendered
Before the axe you bow
Time to pay the Piper friend; your gold can't save you now

- Professor 929

The Blue Collar Way

The Blue Collar Way
Means we live by a code
We have to be strong for we shoulder the load

If we don't deliver
The world will implode
We live in a place where rubber meets road

We must not fail
The stakes are too high
We have to succeed. It's do or die!

When your house is ablaze
We'll be there in a flash
Braving the flames, the smoke, and the ash

We're out on the beat
Waging war on crime
Protecting the innocent time after time

We build the cities
The bridges and streets
We're braving the snow, the rain, and the heat

We're building the schools
The cars and the planes
We're driving the trucks, the ships and the trains

We work for a living
The Blue Collar Way
We get the job done day after day

We do a fine job
Cause our standards are high
We're blue collar proud till the day that we die!

-Professor 929

Team

We have our assignments
Or so it would seem
But we cover each other we're on the same team

We can't all be below
Shoveling coal
It's imperative that each one should know his own role

For this team to succeed
On this perilous trip
Someone must have vision to pilot this ship

We all may contribute
In various ways
This team will grow stronger as we pass through the days

Working united
Achieving the goal
We'll learn one another as the journey unfolds

Fellowship
Is really a treasure
The friends that one keeps is truly his measure

We chart our own destiny
So mind your post well
Our final conclusion only time will tell

- Professor 929

My Sister

My sister, my sister
Please listen to me
I simply must share the game that I see

The world has been cruel
For you bare the scar
Induced to submit and hate what you are

Hiding yourself
Is somewhat unwise
It's hard to be free when you're in disguise

Don't listen to them
Their words are untrue
The merchants have plenty of products for you

They are pushing pills
For you to be thin
How can you be comfortable in your own skin?

Your hair is too short
Your skin is too rough
They're saying that you're just not quite good enough

Wigs and powders
Life giving creams
An insecure heart is a business man's dream

They'll try to finesse you
And play with your head
Exploiting all women until they are dead

These guys are all villains
Demented and sick
Reject all the lies; don't fall for their trick

True beauty, it seems
Can't be found in stores
Embrace all the gifts that are naturally yours

Look in the mirror
Love what you see
It's all about you. It's not about me

-    Professor 929

Neda's Cry

(Neda Agha-Soltan)

I see you my sister
Try not to despair
Oppression's upon you. It just isn't fair!

Their sins are transparent
For you bear the scar
Cowardly impotent men that they are

Seizing control
So you cannot rise
They think your success will mean their demise

Flimsy of ego
It's painfully clear
They wish to suppress you, they act out of fear

So insecure
And fragile of mind
Their actions suggest that they're totally blind

They can't understand
It's out of their reach
They won't absorb wisdom that you try to teach

Filled with contempt
Submission they crave
They want you to live on your knees as a slave

Deplorable cowards
They will never see
The whole world would prosper if you were set free

Their time is at hand
No where can they run
They'll all have to answer for what they have done

So stand tall my sisters
Your freedom is near
Unite and rejoice let go of your fear

I see you my sisters
Believe me I do
Your struggle is valiant. I celebrate you.

- Professor 929

Color

A man is a man
No matter the hue
You can't tell by color just what he might do

A human being's skin
Is just a mere cover
For what lay inside over time you'll discover

Imprudent at best
And really quite small
Prejudging your sister or brother at all

Remember the lesson
We all will discover
We shouldn't be judging a book by its cover

Just look at the pain
And hatred it's wrought
A double-edged snare, do not become caught

History teaches
That bias is wrong
We are a great family where all do belong

Discrimination
Must not be our way
Racism is evil! What more can I say?

-    Professor 929
                    -

They

There they go again
Right there on the news
Always complaining and singing the blues

Carrying pickets
And dissident signs
I think that those people are crossing the line

The world isn't perfect
Everyone knows
If they don't like this country then why don't they go?

We'll be fine without them
Go on and you'll see
If I never see them again that's fine with me

Diversity right!
It's way over rated
The benefits of it are way overstated

If we all were the same
That would be great
No different opinions, or views, or debate

Everyone thinking
And acting the same
Then our world would be quiet, more placid, and tame

But those people can do things
I might miss somewhat
At times it might seem that we're stuck in a rut

They fought by my side
Defending this land
Maybe without them things just might be bland

Less choices of music
And places to eat
Perhaps our world might be a tad incomplete

Perhaps I could listen
To what they might say
Hold on just a minute. Perhaps they should stay!

- Professor 929

The Good Old Days

The good old days
Weren't so good to me
Just step in my shoes
And perhaps you will see

Just stop for a moment
And pull up a chair
You need to consider
Things weren't that fair

Just listen real closely
Please don't make a sound
Hold on to your seat
Whilst I break it on down

In the good old days
They brought us over on ships
They tried to break our spirits
As they beat us with whips

In the good old days
We weren't allowed to read
They would not let us learn
And yet we still succeed

While you were sitting around
Sipping cold lemonade
We were working for free
And we never got paid!

In the good old days
You need to stop and take note
That we were very oppressed
We could not even vote!

In the good old days
When I was very young
If I dared to fight back
Then I would just get hung

In the good old days
There was always a fuss

In the good old days
I rode the back of the bus

In the good old days
We could not even drink
From the fountain in front
We used the colored sink

In the good old days
I fought on the front line
But when I came back home
I could not make a dime

You miss the good old days
'Cause they were good to you
And before we met
You did not have a clue

No, I'm not bitter
Life goes by too fast
I live for the future
Can't dwell in the past

But the old days were trying
Now you know how I feel
My peeps had real struggles
So, I'm keeping it real!

-   Professor 929

The Gray

How I do cherish
The old and the gray
They've learned a great deal back in the day

A wonderful resource
For wisdom I seek
I sit up and listen whenever they speak

I ask for advice
And guidance I need
They honestly want to see me succeed

So they carefully listen
To my every word
They repeat the questions they think that they heard

They use love and wisdom
To help guide my way
I've come to rely on the words that they say

I have greatly prospered
From counsel they give
Making good choices each day that I live

I highly suggest
A chat with the gray
You might be intrigued by what they might say

Sit down and converse
For a good little while
A good conversation might make you both smile

You must listen closely
To all that they say
Receive the wise counsel from the old and the gray

- Professor 929

Patient

I try to be a good a patient
But my patience wares thin
You know what I mean if you've been where I've been

They talk about me
As though I weren't there
Sometimes it would seem like they don't even care

They talk down to me
As if I were a child
They infuriate me but I still remain mild

The Doctor is blind
He will never see
We might get some where if he'd listen to me

The nurse tries to help
They bear such a load
Sometimes they can't help but meltdown and implode

Technicians are jaded
Callused and cold
They are always saying, 'I just do what I'm told!'

The system is backward
And full of red tape
The insurance goblins should be tried for mass rape

It's all about cash
They think I don't know
At times I feel I should just get up and go

I feel disrespected
I just have to cry
My life is in limbo as time passes by

Meanwhile I suffer
Hanging on by a thread
I just stare out the window from my hospital bed

- Professor 929

Trouble

Hey look its trouble
Long time no see
I'm doing well. Are you looking for me?

Well, here I am
With a minute to kill
So, let's get it on. I know the drill

So, what do you have?
The usual game
It's a different day but it's always the same

Trouble at home
Upsetting my wife
Threat to my freedom, or maybe my life

Relative calling
Me on the phone
Desperately hitting me up for a loan

Letter from school
About my kids
Listing the horrible things that they did

Well, whatever it is
I'm sure it's not good!
I'm going to take a pass if you would

Trouble's not really
My cup of tea
I'm trying to float through life hassle free

Trouble is really
A young man's game
Trouble and worry are one in the same

Older and wiser
I see you arrive
Evading the carnage so that I may survive

I'll take my time
And think it all through
Devising a way to neutralize you

I'm not having it
No not today
So, move it along and be on your way

I'll see you next time
You're coming through
Right now, I have much better things to do

- Professor 929

Protect and Serve

You're not hear to protect me
Though that is your job
I receive better treatment from those in the mob

I sometimes get flagged
For driving while dark
So, I pull off the road and put it in park

My hands in your view
I freeze in one spot
You must not be anxious, lest I get shot

"Do you know why I stopped you?"
Yes, I believe I do
You stopped me because I look different from you

So you use that old line
That's clearly fictitious
"I stopped you because you look somewhat suspicious."

I look in your eyes
Suspicious you say?
That's really disturbing. Please tell me, in what way?

"You're not from around here
I just ran your plate
So, why are you here? It's awfully late!"

So you've decided to stop me
Don't think I belong?
I live on this block. Your info is wrong!

Here is my license
My address and name?
Then I look at you sadly as your tone starts to change.

"Senator Johnson?"
Yes sir that is me
I was just on the news today. Didn't you see?

The Mayor and I
Really go back
He's just like my brother as a matter of fact

I'll make sure I call him
About this here stop
He might just consider retraining his cops

You look kind of ill
Son, are you alright?
If you are quite through, I'll bid you good night!

- Professor 929

Justice

I know for a fact
Justice is not blind
For those without wealth the courts are unkind

The system's designed
To rob you of hope
The concept itself is a slippery slope

We know by now
Don't trust the police
They will never learn; 'No justice, no peace!'

Some lawyers themselves
Are as guilty as sin
They do not seek truth; they're just here to win

The judge is imperfect
So you'd better pray
You may be abused if they've had a bad day

The system is flawed
It's too imprecise
A game of mere chance, a role of the dice!

What's really disturbing
And tragically sad
Is our courts are the best that mankind's ever had!

Don't enter this circus
You just may be lost
Take my advice, stay out at all cost!

- Professor 929

Lost in the Hype

Don't rest for a moment
It's time to make haste
To lose this key battle would be such a waste

For years we've been trying
To help those in need
Now we're right on the brink this time we'll succeed

The suits will not quit
They're still in the fight
They provoke and accuse and try to incite

They have been exposed
They have made it plain
They will stop at nothing to derail this train

The issues they raise
Are but an illusion
Their goal is to perpetrate utter confusion

Don't listen to babble
That is not sincere
We must remain focused, productive and clear

Don't misunderstand
We all have some gripe
But we must remain true, don't get lost in the hype

- Professor 929

Election

I have some free time
So, I'll kick off my shoes
Ease back in my chair
And turn on the news

A flame broiled steak
And an ice cold beer
I start to relax
And I keep the snacks near

Time for the circus
I mean the election
It sickens us all
Just like an infection

Panelists shouting
All bothered and mad
Utter buffoonery
Wretchedly sad

Distortion of facts
By all of these suits
They smirk at the chaos
They think that they're cute

Do you not see it?
The game that is played
Just follow the money
And see who gets paid

It is prostitution
Just stop and consider
They do sell themselves
To the highest bidder

We're being betrayed
Of this there's no doubt
You do understand?
They're selling us out!

They blow through the cash
At a dizzying pace
They'll smile at the camera
And lie to your face

Political warfare
It's just a smoke screen
Government for the people?
It was a great dream!

The government serves those
With money and power
If you are poor
This is a dark hour

The poor need some help
Their futures look grim
Will no one step up?
Who'll lobby for them?

But there is this new guy
Not like the rest
He seems to be focused
On doing his best

He seems to have vision
And has great appeal
Can he bring about change?
Only time will reveal

- Professor 929

Peep the Game

Peep the game people
Peep the game
This world is gripped by greed. You know it's a shame!

Our brothers are starving
While we turn them away
Babies are dying, forty thousand each day

Powers don't care
About the poor
It's all about greed they always want more

They pollute our air
And ruin our seas
They're killing our planet just like a disease

Their lies are insane
Tired and old
They're selling us out for more silver and gold

They lie to your face
And you just take it
You just sit around and let them fake it

Well I have had it!
Enough is enough
I'm ready to struggle, knuckle down and get rough

I'll turn up the heat
To unknown degrees
My plan is to bring them all down to their knees

My mission is simple
Exposing the game
The curtain will perish; destruction by flame

When it is over
They will be no more
There will be no tyrants to feast on the poor

- Professor 929

The Hustle

I call it 'The Hustle'
Much more than a dance
A game of the ages, you don't stand a chance

Out on the hunt
I move like a shark
Diabolical menace, I lurk in the dark

Ambitious and crafty
My motive is greed
I get you to crave all the things you don't need

I target the young
They just cannot see
I toy with their hearts. They're no match for me

Deceit is my creed
It is a disgrace
I'll flash you a smile and lie to your face

I promise the world
While crushing your health
Your purchase contributes to growing my wealth

Out on the prowl
I'm studying you
I lie and I cheat; that's just what I do

I cannot be stopped
While running my game
I may be the rogue, but you are the blame

You fail to distinguish
The wrong from the right
The truth of the game is beyond your sight

I have you so twisted
You insolent sap
You think you are free while caught in my trap

Selling you out;
Incredibly sleazy
At times I can't believe it's so easy

Whispering softly
Into your ear
I sing you the songs that you long to hear

Promising all
The things that you crave
Turning you into my misguided slave

The art of illusion
I bait, then I switch
Robbing you blind is making me rich

You lust for the lie
The facts are dismissed
Believing it's that, when really it's this

I've captured your mind
And crippled your brain
You're eagerly dressing in shackles and chain

Deeply ensnared
In my little game
Proudly displaying my designer name

I've branded the masses
For all to see
Make no mistake, they belong to me

I send them to work
In homes and in schools
Strategically planted seducing more fools

Shallow and empty
Sexy and fresh
Exploiting your weakness by peddling flesh

Weaving a web
That's flawlessly planned
Bringing you down by own your foolish hand

It works every time
The same tired trick
I set out the bait then real you in quick

My gullible puppet
I put you on sale
You pull in more victims. This stuff never fails!

Eroding your spirit
While exploiting you
I'll wring out your heart, and then break it in two

Your actions result
In sealing your fate
Someday you'll catch on, but by then it's too late

In front of the mirror
You'll open your eyes
You have become something you used to despise

You let me entice you
You knew it was wrong
You chose to be weak when you should have been strong

You wanted to party
And now you are lost
Lamenting the outcome while paying the cost

Completely defeated
And scorched by the sun
Used and abused, and now you are done

I'm finished with you
So take your last bow
I'm stalking your children and their babies now

I'll get in their heads
And make them my slaves
They'll live on their knees and crawl to their graves

You set the example
They're following you
They heard what you said, but they see what you do

Lost and turned out
Your failure's complete
Watching your children at work on the street

And so it's a wrap
I thank you my friend
For me it's been fun, for you it's the end.

-Professor 929

Why

Why ask why?
Scoundrels may ask
Why do you seek to take me to task?

Why not accept things...
Just as they are?
You question too much. You take it too far.

Is there something...
You have to say?
Do you really believe there's a better way?

Why yes I do
As a matter of fact
Your values are broken, perverted, and cracked

Why are there not more...
With something to say?
Why do we relent to the wicked today?

Why do we not rise?
Stand up and fight
Why is it, that we won't demand what is right?

People today
Wanting of soul
Why are we not fearless, united and bold?

Why not speak out?
Why not take a stand?
Why not remove those who oppress our land?

I'll question it all
Till the day that I die
With perennial faith in the power of why

- Professor 929

Gangster?

Wannabe gangsters
You still around?
Walking the streets with your pants sagging down

You look just like clowns
But that's not really news
Though you need the red nose, and some big floppy shoes

A life of crime
Seems some what appealing?
Trafficking drugs, robbing and stealing?

I know you don't listen
So I'm going to shout
Stop playing around; get in or stay out!

Wannabe gangster
Go get a job
Son, you could never survive in the mob!

If you don't change
You're going to jail
Praying that someone delivers your bail

What a surprise
Nobody came
Your boys have completely forgotten your name

What is that smell?
Is that what I think?
Go take a shower 'cause' you really stink

Head to the shower
Take some protection
Grown men are ready to show you affection

I'm warning you son
This could be you
If you keep acting the way that you do

If I catch you once more
Blocking the street
I'm going to make sure I run over your feet.

Thought you were a man
I took that for granted
You're the sorriest skirt wearing punk on the planet!

- Professor 929

Enough!

That was really uncool
Why'd you tell that lie?
You don't even care that you made that girl cry?

Have you lost your mind?
You never make sense
You can't have a laugh at lady's expense!

You need some correction
'Cause' you don't have a clue
I'm going to break it on down, 'cause' its way overdue

It seems to us all
That you never stop drinking
'Cause' you always start talking without even thinking!

Sometimes it would seem
Like you've been smoking grass
'Cause' you get in a crowd and you never show class!

Your manners are horrid
You act like a joke
Sometimes you act like you've been snorting coke!

You act like a monster
With no self control
No kidding my friend you act like a troll!

Can't be around women
Cause you always stare
I'm done with you man. I will take you nowhere!

You better be careful
Don't make me get rough
I'm telling you now son enough is enough!

- Professor 929

More than Just a Name

You call yourself "Hova"
Is this some kind of joke?
Profanity, bravado and some artificial smoke!

You took what is not yours
It's looking somewhat grim
You'll have to face your Maker. You'll have to answer Him!

Have you lost your mind?
Did you really think this through?
This is not a game son. What are you going to do?

You must be in a bubble
You must not have a clue
Can you give salvation to the ones who worship you?

You've overstepped your realm
Your actions are bazaar
You need to reassess yourself. You're taking it too far!

You need to listen closely
I don't begrudge your fame
But you have blundered gravely. It's more than just some name.

Are you the Almighty?
The One who's in control?
Do you possess the power to restore one fallen soul?

Where were you my friend?
When time itself began?
Are you some kind of spirit, or just some puny man?

Can you end all sadness?
Put an end to strife?
Do you possess the secret to bestow the breath of life?

You have been admonished
I hope you feel remorse
Renounce your prior actions. You must reverse your course!

- Professor 929

No

Hear my man
Without a word to say
Living minute to minute and day to day

He doesn't speak
For he has no voice
No words, no option, no out and no choice

No house, no home
No time to play
Nowhere to run and no place to stay

A hard path to walk
A hard life to live
Hard to forget, and harder to forgive

No one will help
They won't take a stand
No open doors, or hearts, nor hands

There is no shelter
You know it's not right
No place of comfort in the middle of the night

No escape
From the blistering heat
No faith, no fun and nothing to eat

No government agent
To stop the abuse
No logic, no reason, there is no excuse

No understanding
From the police
If there is no justice, there can be no peace

He lives in a prison
It will never cease
No light, no mercy, no early release

Days move slowly
Life goes fast
He has no future for he has no past

Out on the edge
A lone outcast
You know in your heart that he's not going to last

He's out on the corner
Only here for a time
His days are number like the words in this rhyme

There is no joy
As his life fades away
No liberation at the end of the day

No love for my brother
Until his life ends
No change, no money, no help and no friends

No compassion
As the world passes by
And then he is gone in the blink of an eye

-Professor 929

Yes

Yes I will practice
The Golden rule
At work, at play, at home, in school

Yes, if I can
I will give you more
Yes to the hungry, the weak and the poor

Yes to the people
The young and the old
Yes to the wise, the fearless, the bold

Yes to tomorrow
A much better way
Yes to the promise of a much brighter day

Yes to the masses
Facing unrest
Yes to the needy and the oppressed

Yes to the tired
Without a bed
Yes to the babies who are crying for bread

Without restraint
Compelled share
Yes I'll protect you because I do care

Yes I have love
For all those I meet
The doctor, the student, the girl on the street

The fallen, the moral
The man in the ditch
The harlot, the hustler, the poor and the rich

The dreamers, the builders
The singer of songs
The righteous, the sinners, meek and the strong

Yes to the lovers
Right from the start
The high and the mighty, the lowly of heart

The yellow, the red
The black and the white
Yes to the ones who are wanting of sight

Yes to the people
All over the land
Divided we fell, united we'll stand

Yes my friend
I'll always believe
It is better to give than it is to receive

-Professor 929

Dreamer

To realize your destiny
You must pay the cost
Accepting the harshness of innocence lost

The world is not perfect
I tell you my friend
The way that we live is truly a sin

Merely existing
Is just not the way
We find that we die just a little each day

A sea of despair
We struggle to cope
Devoid of a future, direction or hope

Contemptuous masses
Or so it would seem
They will try to hurt you and crush all your dreams

Defeated and broken
Their future unclear
With nothing to lose they lash out in fear

They don't really hate you
They have lost their way
They gave up their hopes and their dreams yesterday

You can make a difference
Don't give up the fight
Chase all your dreams with all of your might

Fruition is key
Dreams do insight
Encouraging those who gave up the fight

You are a rare breed
Your numbers are few
The world is much better with dreamers like you

- Professor 929

Spiritual

"You need to decide
You need to come clean
There's no middle ground, there's no in
between

Judgment is coming
With full recompense
You must be decisive, get off of the fence!"

Jehovah

The most powerful power
In the whole of the whole
Omnipotent Master, the Almighty Soul

You are the Master
Of all of the arts
The Hearer of Prayers, the Reader of Hearts

You reside on a throne
In the heavens above
I am overwhelmed at the depth of your love

I struggle to fathom
The scope of your power
I ponder creation hour by hour

My awe of you grows
As time passes by
Immersed in the glory of the midnight sky

I thank you Dear Father
For Your merciful ways,
Bountiful blessings and the length of the days

Thank You for woman,
The feminine touch
Thank you for family we love them so much

You've given us beauty
And vision to see
Thank You for all that You've given to me

My passion for Thee
Cannot be undone
I sing You this praise in the name of Your Son

- Professor 929

Father

My Father in Heaven
I love you so dear
I draw ever closer as your day draws near

I ask that you keep on
Providing the light
I ask that you help me refine my insight

I ask for your Spirit
To strengthen my soul
I must remain loyal, courageous and bold

Your masterful plans
Can't be interrupted
Your purpose for mankind cannot be corrupted

I am so imperfect
I sin everyday
I rely on your word to show me the way

I ask you for mercy
I try to do right
But when I fall short I'm truly contrite

Cold winds are now blowing
Please do keep me warm
Protect me from evil and darkness and harm

This world is so evil
It brings about stress
I ask that you bless those under duress

I thank you Dear Father
For loving me so
Thanks for the time you've allowed me to grow

You have made me ready
I'm steady of nerve
I bow down before you; I'm ready to serve!

- Professor 929

Creator

In the still of the night
Not a cloud in the sky
The air is so cool, so crisp and so dry

I look to the Heavens
My view's crystal clear
I stop to marvel at the bright little sphere

Off in the distance
I think I see Mars
I peer even deeper and I gaze at the stars

As I drink in the beauty
My thoughts start to wander
In a moment of focus my mind starts to ponder

How did this happen?
It can't be by chance
Did this all just appear by mere happenstance?

The stars are in motion
They will never cease
They move with precision just like a timepiece

Consider our planet
So blue and alive
So perfectly formed life can't help but thrive

Such a well-balanced home
The birth place of mankind
From a logical view our world seems well designed

Such a curious notion
Just look at your hand
Open your heart and you may understand

That we're not here by chance
But there's nothing to fear
There must be a Creator, for me it is clear!

Professor 929

Thank You

I thank the Creator
For Heaven and Earth
I thank you for being
And the day of my birth

Thank you for life
And the days that you give
Thank you for laughter
And the freedom to live

Thanks for my mind
Crafted with skill
The power to choose
The gift of free will

Thank you for mercy
And tender affection
A mere image of you
I am your reflection

Thank you for faith
To carry me through
Thanks for your word
Which always proves true

Thank you for hope
To keep my heart whole
Thanks for your spirit
Refreshing my soul

Thank you for love
All said and done
You so loved the world
You gave up your son

Thank you Jehovah
For all of these things
Your many rich blessings
And all that they bring

- Professor 929

Crossroads

A perplexing dilemma
At the crossroads of time
A decision to make and the burden is mine

All of these paths
Have no end in sight
It's hard to decide which path would be right

I will take my time
There's no room for haste
To make a mistake would be such a waste

I pull out the map
And study it long
I just can't afford a decision that's wrong

The map indicates
The path that is best
It's the narrow road, over there, up on the left

I start down that path
I know that it's right
For the farther I go, the clearer my sight

So now I am happy
To shoulder this load
I have made the right choice at the fork in the road

- Professor 929

Walking the Path

Walking the path
Can be hard to do
Committing to something that's greater than you

Keep pressing on
No time to rest
Beware of pitfalls on this arduous quest

Trouble ahead
Is a fair bet
When the rains come, plan to get wet

Try to stay faithful
Pray when you can
Remember, you're only an imperfect man

Groping in darkness
Is better to do
When you have brothers who will walk with you

Study your subject
Knowledge is key
Lighting the pathway for all men to see

When you draw close
To the end of it all
Try to stay standing, lest you should fall

When you are finished
Your journey is through
Take a deep breath, and enjoy the view!

- Professor 929

Tribulation

As I observe the horizon
Dark clouds start to form
Tribulation is coming
I must weather this storm

I've had time to get ready
For this most dreaded day
I'll soon see what I'm made of
I shall not run away

I've created a punch list
Of the things I must do
First I'll pray for the strength
That will carry me through

I will stick to the plan
I will come out alive
I will be altruistic
I'll help others survive

It's all out of my hands
Though it helps to be brave
I'll pray for mercy
Lest no flesh will be saved

We all have a commission
And we must see it through
We must all draw together
When the battle ensues

When the battle is over
We will all see the Son
We will build a New World
A new day has begun

- Professor 929

The Prize

Since the Lord is our Shepherd
Know this to be true
Let's get with the program, we know what to do

The end is coming
And it won't be late
Though we don't know the minute, the hour, the date

While there is still time
Let's right all of our wrongs
Help others to get up, walk upright, and grow strong

Spread the good news
That the Prince has been here
For all true of heart their salvation is near

Be good to each other
Be loving and wise
And remember to keep your eyes on the prize

We'll shoulder our load
I know that we can
If you need some help, I'll lend you a hand

If life seems too much
At the end of the day
Remember our blessings and bow down to pray

He will hear and strengthen us
Carry us through
He listens to me, He'll listen to you

The end is coming
Like a thief in the night
But you still have some time
So, fight the good fight

- Professor 929

Let It Go

Anger has seduced you
You need to be aware
You need to proceed wisely. This path is but a snare

Who am I to judge?
I've made mistakes before
I just don't want to see you caught up in a costly war

I know you demand justice
I know you need respect
But vengeance is a bitter road. Revenge is not correct

Take time to consider
Take some time to think
Take a breath my friend, and ease back from the brink

You must regain your senses
You must maintain control
You must apply some logic. You've got to slow your roll

Let time work its magic
Let cooler heads prevail
And thus avoid the torment of a public epic fail

Peace unto you
You shall not fall this day
Leave this trap behind you and be upon your way

Wisdom is the key
That opens many doors
When you proceed wisely the victory is yours

Embrace the situation
Allow yourself to grow
Always take the high road, and let that anger go

- Professor 929

Beware

Beware of the Evil
Do not become prey
When you know you should leave he'll convince you to stay

He's been craftily plotting
For eons of time
He is a manslayer; the inventor of crime

He's been known to appear
As an Angel of light
He's masterfully cunning; he'll make wrong seem right

He dwells here among us
We all see the signs
He's increased his efforts for he hasn't much time

Your future is balanced
On the edge of a knife
He will try to deceive and deprive you of life

I am warning you now
'Cause' I want you to see
Please do understand that you're precious to me

To protect you from harm
That is my ambition
To sound the alarm is my sacred commission

Evil is mighty
Would you agree?
But we all have a Friend who is greater than he

Our Friend is a fortress
Seek him out today
He will give you insight and keep evil at bay

Our Friend is Almighty
And free from all blame
When you need protection just call on His name!

Professor 929

Believe

A few humble words
On Matthew 24
Open your mind, prepare to explore

A battle is brewing
It draws ever near
Prepare yourself wisely soon it will appear

The Kingdom is coming
Now everyone knows
Some will follow though most will oppose

The King is immortal
He will not loose
It's time to step up, everybody must choose

You need to decide
You need to come clean
There's no middle ground, there's no in between

Judgment is coming
With full recompense
You must be decisive, get off of the fence

Are these the last days?
Perhaps, the last hour?
Learn with much haste for knowledge is power

We won't know the hour
These words will hold true
Take heed of this warning, I'm pleading with you

The Devil is doomed
The battle will prove
It's all academic checkmate in one move

The Shepherd will lead you
The price has been paid
Follow his footsteps, do not be afraid

Satan will test you
He works to deceive
Hold onto your faith, you've got to believe

- Professor 929

It

(A riddle)

Insidious dragon
Slayer of dreams
Lord of destruction
Purveyor of screams

It resides on the earth
Since the dawn of mankind
From the day of ones birth
Our paths are intertwined

Destroyer of hearts
Deplorable crime
It can take worlds apart
A mere piece at a time

It's the darkness of ages
Though I won't let it blind me
It's the builder of cages
I must not let it bind me

It is vulnerable
To the power of light
It cannot survive
Without cover of night

You can defeat *It*
With the sword of truth
Though it's best to start training
When you are a mere youth

Prepare yourself wisely
Study at length
For the wiser you grow
The greater your strength

Teach with haste!
Help others to see!
In time *It* will die!
Then our world will be free!

Professor 929

152

Rain

My heart and soul are tortured
I can't escape my past
If I can't find peace there's no way I'm going to last

So I bow down to my Father
Can you send some relief please?
I ask him for some mercy as I rest upon my knees

I hear some thunder cracking
As I open up one eye
I see a storm a brewing where the mountains kiss the sky

The thunder's getting louder
For its coming right this way
The storm is coming to me but I think I'm going to stay

My mind was in tailspin
I was hanging by a thread
These droplets are a godsend as they fall upon my head

I look up at my Father
As I kneel here in the rain
I know he sent this storm to wash away my pain

The water has engulfed me
And yet I'm feeling warm
I start to feel lighthearted as I embrace this storm

Completely saturated
I'm soaked from head to toe
Now it seems I'm ready to let all my worries go

I've got to thank my Father
For the gift he sent to me
He washed away my troubles for his rain has set me free

This storm is very soothing
Don't think that I'm insane
There is nothing like a shower in the cool refreshing rain

- Professor 929

Reflection

Your life in review
The final inspection
An appropriate moment for deep introspection

It's your judgment day
No kidding my friend
To see where you're going, let's look where you've been

Have you accomplished...
All of your dreams?
Figured out life? What does it mean?

What about power, prestige and wealth?
Would you give them all up?
If it meant perfect health

What about people?
Any regrets?
Did you show any love to the strangers you met?

Have a clean conscience?
Do any dirt?
Is there a soul you intended to hurt?

If you went back
What would you change?
Any priorities you'd rearrange?

What about people?
Would they come first?
Give water to those dying of thirst?

What do you say...
To a new circumstance?
Would you do better if given a chance?

You've been granted more time
So says the court
Better get it together. Your time's getting short!

- Professor 929

Righteous Fury

For a spiritual man
Loving peace is a must
But defending the meek is a cause that is just

Strife is unpleasant
I'm sure you'll agree
But we must take a stand if we want to live free

Don't flee from the tyrant
Who perpetrates wrong
Instead, go right at him with hammer and tong

You must be aggressive
Put him on the spot
Remember to strike while the iron is hot

You must show no weakness
He will pick you apart
Look into to his eyes and snatch out his heart

In the heat of the moment
You're both judge and jury
Conducting yourself with a righteous fury

When correcting your brother
You must not be cruel
Remember to practice The Golden Rule

It's wise to be gracious
When the battle is won
Take heed of these words and you'll prosper my son

- Professor 929

How Long Must We Suffer

How long must we suffer...
The wages of sin?
How long will we battle the fruit of bad men?

How long must we wander...
With burden to bear?
How long must we languish in utter despair?

How long will we resist...
The bread of the swine?
How long can we survive while holding the line?

What will it take...
For the people to rise?
What must occur to open your eyes?

How long will hatred...
Tear us apart?
What words must be spoken to soften your heart?

What will it take...
To compel you to care?
What must you witness to move you to share?

Can you be reached...
With love and affection?
Can you move forth in a better direction?

We continue to bear
The weight of the load
How long must we travel this treacherous road?

- Professor 929

Zion

(Ephesians 6:14-17)

Zion is in me
In front and behind
Much more than a nation, it's the state of my mind

My focus is clear
No questions I ask
I'm eager to get right down to the task

I am resolute
I will never yield
The truth is my sword and my faith is my shield

I shall not retreat
No mater the pain
With fiery heart and ice in my veins

To battle I trod
Fearless and bold
With eyes like an eagle steely and cold

My rival is evil
He taunts me to war
I know the outcome. I know what's in store

Malevolent tyrant
Slayer of men
Lord of deception, father of sin

His fate has been sealed
The price has been paid
He will taste defeat by the edge of the blade

The evil has fallen
For all now to see
My soul has been lifted, the world is now free!

- Obsidian 929

Romance

"You reach into me
  With beautiful eyes
  My innermost man now secretly cries

  You've captured my heart
  I give you control
  You've moved me to tears and shaken my soul"

Moments

(Ode to the Masseuse)

Moment by moment
My life starts to slow
My mind is at peace as I start to let go

I enter a space
That's truly sublime
I start to relax with the passage of time

I have left the world
It just does not matter
I'm free from all chaos and meaningless chatter

Enter the Master
To show me the way
You now work my soul like a sculptor works clay

Your fingers are soothing
Just like a warm rain
I inhale the pleasure and exhale the pain

Your magical hands
Sing an Angelic song
You may be petite but your powers are strong

Silently working
With not much to say
You've skillfully washed all my worries away

I am truly grateful
For your expertise
I exit your temple my soul now at ease

This moment is precious
It belongs to me
I savor this moment for now I am free

Professor 929

Lips

Irresistibly charming
Your sensuous smile
Invites me to come and relax for a while

Slowly approaching
We kiss as we meet
I savor your lips as I bask in your heat

Whenever we kiss
My body unwinds
Leaving the cares of the world behind

Sumptuous lips
Delectable treat
So round, so soft and deliciously sweet

I hunger for you
For I am your man
Tasting your lips just as long as I can

I'm hopelessly lost
What more can I say
I find myself blissfully drifting away

Drowning in passion
We are in a zone
The moment solicits a sigh and a moan

Your wondrous lips
Have captured my sight
Completely consumed in the heat of the night

Time disappears
I can't comprehend
Kissing your lips for hours on end

Standing together
My hands on your hips
Absorbing the warmth of the love from your lips

- Professor 929

Fingertips

Fingertips
Upon my skin
Stoking the fires that smolder within

Fingertips
They are not mine
Messaging my flesh, they tingle my spine

So gentle and sure
Loving and just
Your fingertips convey a devoted trust

Masterfully skilled
Your senses are sharp
Stroking my soul like the strings of a harp

You reach in to me
And caress my heart
Your fingertips reveal a nurturing art

Warmly seductive
Your touch is complete
Your fingertips exude a sensual heat

Your fingertips move me
I need you so much
The air is electric whenever we touch

Inclined to submit
To your fingertips
I sigh as your fingers encircle my lips

They carry me off
On rapturous trips
I transcend this world through your fingertips

- Professor 929

Kiss

Beauty in motion
A most splendid view
At moments you seem too good to be true

I implore you to speak
With your warm gentle voice
We two are as one in love, and by choice

Though you're perfectly formed
Know this to be true
You excel in compassion and intellect too

As I look in your eyes
My heart starts to dance
I 'm helplessly falling right into a trance

I draw you to me
As your lips meet mine
Our hearts beat as one for a moment in time

A man and a woman
Locked face to face
Passion we share in a tender embrace

Food for my soul
Whenever we kiss
It elevates me to a heavenly bliss

A kiss for the ages
Priceless in worth
A kiss such as this could move heaven and earth

- Professor 929

Dream

As time ambles forth
My appetite grows
My thoughts fall upon you. My heart itself slows

A calm overtakes me
I'm filled with a peace
My mind is at ease as time has just ceased

I have closed my eyes
Though I am not blind
The image of you firmly fixed in my mind

I fade into slumber
I have fallen deep
My mind is awake though I am fast asleep

I delve into images
Lucid and clear
I walk with you love, though you are not here

You reach out to me
And sing me a song
Your voice is angelic, enchanting and strong

You reach into me
With beautiful eyes
My innermost man now secretly cries

You've captured my heart
I give you control
You've moved me to tears and shaken my soul

This is an illusion
Or so it would seem
I will always cherish this ravishing dream

- Professor 929

163

Touch

The touch of your hand
Moves me to tears
You have soothed the scars I've earned through the years

Gentle yet firm
Your touch proves to be
I shall not misstep with your light to guide me

Your passion has freed me
Of the weights that I bear
I gladly surrender to your tender care

Given to you
Without hesitation
My heart's in your hands with no reservation

I stand incomplete
Without your caress
You dissipate angst with skillful finesse

I need you beloved
You have to believe
As vital to me as the air that I breathe

The haven of love
I do crave so much
I long for the warmth and the truth of your touch

- Professor 929

Heat

In the still of the night
We are finally alone
We light a few candles and turn off the phone

I am quite intrigued
By your devilish grin,
Your beautiful hair and your buttery skin

You slowly approach
With that look in your eye
You give me a wink. I give you a sigh.

Consuming your heat
Through your warm finger tips
I delve into your eyes as I taste your sweet lips

Your whisper is magic
Your lips to my ear
I feel your soft breath as I pull you in near

You've rendered me speechless
For what can I say?
I lift you up gently to take you away

Besieged by your splendor
You are my delight
Your body aglow in the warm candlelight

We are intertwined
Alone and complete
We never cool off for we make our own heat

- Professor 929

Nubian

Nubian Beauty
With the raven hair
Eyes like the night without compare

Queen of the ages
Mother of man
Skin smooth as silk, and perfectly tanned

Sauntering gate
Curvaceous hips
Radiant smile upon fully formed lips

Conquering hearts
As you amble by
Inciting a passion no man could deny

Your scent is hypnotic
Your look is exotic
Your sensual style is somewhat erotic

Your speech sooths the soul
A melodious song
I crave to be near you all day long

Fiercely loyal
With timeless charm
I'll protect you my queen, you shall see no harm

Urbane wisdom
Complex and refined
International treasure to the whole of mankind

A fiery soul
From the land of the Nile
With your beauty and grace and your Nubian style

- Professor 929

Empress

Empress of the Orient
So glad that you are here
Please come and lay right next to me, I long to have you near

Subtle and soft spoken
You move with such grace
You float across the room in a most deliberate pace

Mystery surrounds you
As I peer into your eyes
I find you irresistible I have been hypnotized

Delicate in stature
You've chosen to reveal
Pressure cannot break you. Your spirit is of steel

Like a budding flower
Closed surreptitiously
Slowly you have blossomed forth, you are revealed to me

To most you are a riddle
They barely know your name
Your heart is quite well hidden, and thus it shall remain

Concealed from the world
Others cannot see
The fiery hot passion you have reserved for me

As I caress your body
You draw ever near
You melt into my soul as I whisper in your ear

You cannot be conquered
You will always be free
Your love's a precious treasure and you've given it to me

-    Professor 929

Wisdom

Once upon a time
In a land far away
There lived a young lad
With not much to say

Humble and eager
To learn all he could
He did pray for wisdom
And he tried to do good

He learned as he listened
To words of his day
He learned from all people
The young and the gray

As time moved on
The young man grew wise
His name became known
Much to his surprise

Nobles would travel
From mysterious lands
They sailed across oceans
And trekked across sands

They queried intensely
By day and by night
The answers he gave
Would prove his insight

They could not confound him
They would if they could
They had to admit
All his answers were good

Then one day a question
From a woman of fame
Her eyes were like emeralds
Her hair was like flame

I've only one question
That I must ask of you

What's the greatest of deeds that all people can do?

He smiled then he answered
It is written my queen
We must love one another
And keep our hearts clean

She paused for a moment
Then let out a smile
She was quite impressed
So, she stayed for a while

She kept asking questions
And he answered them right
They kept right on talking
Late into the night

They talked with each other
Day after day
A bond grew between them
So he asked her to stay

She wept as she answered
The answer was YES!
The two became one
And their union was blessed

They live in a castle
Across the great sands
And they still answer questions
From faraway lands

- Professor 929

Room with a View

This is a splendid setting
In a most attractive place
This room was decorated with the most exquisite taste

The floors are made of marble
The fixtures are all brass
The view is quite splendid for the walls are made of glass

In the master bedroom
There sits a golden bed
The sheets are all white linen and they're trimmed with golden tread

We have to get some dinner
For now it's almost eve
But this room is so fantastic neither of us wants to leave

So we'll be dinning in tonight
This ambiance ideal
We'll order some room service and we'll share a quite meal

The dinner was outrageous
Almost too good to be true
But my favorite thing about it was spending time with you

When our meal is over
We look out from on high
We hear the seagulls singing as they float across the sky

We see a couple walking
Where the water meets the sand
We smile at one another as I reach to hold your hand

We share this special moment
As I stand here next to you
We marvel at the sun set from our room with a view

- Professor 929

House by the Sea

I have heartbreaking news
I got the call today
We have to go to war
I have to go away

I have to leave you now
But know that I'll be back
The power of your love
Will keep my soul in tact

This is a tortured time
I have become withdrawn
I keep on loosing friends
As the days keep dragging on

I've seen some evil things
War takes it way too far
I'll never be the same
I'll always bear this scar

Your letters kept me sane
And now my tour is through
We chart a course for home
I soon will be with you

I've gone to hell and back
My soul has suffered harm
I have returned home
Into your loving arms

I look into your eyes
Can't tell you how I feel
I have been rendered speechless
Please hold me as I heal

Now we're standing here
There's only you with me
Just loving one another
In our house by the sea

- Professor 929

Gallery

The world is my art gallery
With beauty all around
A study in diversity breathtakingly profound

A stroll through the crowd
Reveals astounding art
Sculptures set in motion bring a smile to my heart

I am thus overjoyed
At the visions I see
The greatest art collection and admission's always free

So many shapes and sizes
A variety of hue
Each one a masterpiece almost too good to be true

Deference to the Artist
The Maestro is supreme
I hold the Master Sculptor in superlative esteem

No two works alike
Extraordinarily attractive
The works in this collection are uniquely interactive

I'm always fascinated
Every time I arrive
This exhibit is dynamic and incredibly alive

There are so many beauties
It's too much to digest
I have to take a moment just to give my eyes a rest

I feel so very privileged
To roam this gallery
Though at times I get the feeling that the art is watching me

- Professor 929

Hello

I'm afraid to approach you
What a pitiful crime!
I just sit and think of you for oodles of time

Sadly I daydream
Of being with you
I won't show my feelings but you must have some clue

Seeing your smile
Brightens my day
I wish I could find the right words to say

That I'm very fond of you
I think that you're great
Perhaps, I could take you out on a date!

But that just cannot happen
I'm really quite shy
The thought of it all makes me want to cry

Here you come again
I'll get out of your way
I will remain silent with nothing to say

You're headed right for me
There's no time to hide
You smile on approach with your confident stride

And now here you stand
Looking me in the eye
My heart is exploding as I let out a sigh

Extending your hand
As you start to speak
I hold your hand firmly as my knees get weak

'I've seen you around
And I like your style
Do mind if we sit and just talk for a while?'

- Professor 929

Eyes

I have been richly treated
By an unexpected prize
I have been warmly greeted by a pair of striking eyes

Windows to a universe
I'm driven to explore
Consumed by curiosity; intrigued I must learn more

Your eyes are as the ocean
Superb they overwhelm
So vast and filled with beauty, I dive into your realm

Enchanting and mysterious
Perfectly profound
Your eyes have spoken volumes though you utter not a sound

Radiant and brilliant
Your eyes possess a light
You have a cleaver twinkle like the stars above at night

I have been captivated
I cannot break this trance
I am completely immersed in this visual romance

Consumed by adoration
For your beautiful perfection
I have to break away from this ocular inspection

Returning to my senses
I have become aware
I am somewhat embarrassed for I did not mean to stare

Without a hesitation
I gaze upon the floor
I wish that I could vanish, as I move toward the door

I steal a parting glance
To see your smiling eyes
You reach to stop my exit, what a startling surprise!

Gracefully you hold my arm
You lead me now to walk
Impishly you query, "Do you have some time to talk?"

- Professor 929

The Warmest Ray

Was a Thursday night
On the ninth of July
Almost 11 when you came floating by

Dearest, Ramona how I love your name
Ramona it's clear there's no shame in your game

Your smile is like sunshine
Eyes like the night
Your skin is so smooth, so supple, and bright

Your step is so cool
You could never be cold
Your voice is so warm, inviting, and bold

Fresh off of the breeze
Refreshing are you
These words are sincere, so humble, and true

When you brought out the coffee
I had to look up
And tenderly say, "Thank you so much!"

Exceptional presence
With the warmest of eyes
What a breath of fresh air, and a pleasant surprise

Like the warmth from the sun
You brightened my day
To me you are clearly 'The Warmest Ray'

Ramona, Ramona
I'll be back for more
Coffee from you is worth waiting for

Ramona, Ramona, Ramona...

- Professor 929

Beauty

I gaze upon beauty
With pride and delight
For this battered soul you're a most welcomed sight

You're very much a lady
You exude class and grace
You are a complex woman far more than a pretty face

You have caught me by surprise
That twinkle in your eye
Is somewhat inviting, enchanting and sly

Things in my life
Are painfully wrong
Another time, another place I would step to you strong

Things as they are
I raise the alarm
I'll not be the brother who's world brings you harm

Let me tell you my sister
You are far too fine
To put up with drama least of all mine

Please don't even think
Of me in that way
Keep right on moving, don't linger, don't stay

I cannot love
My heart is a stone
For now it is my destiny to walk my path alone

You're bright and so fresh
Your presence a glow
I'd never expose you to the hell that I know

Any man would be thrilled
To have you in his life
If he saw what I see he would make you his wife

I'm glad that I have met you
I truly love your style
Perhaps we'll meet again someday and sit and chat and smile

- Professor 929

Woman

An Artist made woman,
Truly the best!
Evolution you say?
Surely you jest!

Voluptuous curves,
From her neck to her thighs
As a subject of art brings a tear to my eyes

All shapes and all sizes
In all of her splendor
The feminine form
What a wonderful gender!

The female intellect
An enigma for me
Though a joy to explore, just try it, you'll see

Just stop for a moment
And chat for a while
Gaze into her eyes, gain warmth from her smile

A confident lady knows that she's complete
From the top of her head
To the soles of her feet

A woman unfettered
As free as a dove
A magnificent site,
A real gift from above.

- Professor 929

She

Behold the splendor
Of a beauty refined
An absolute woman unbound by design

Her form is complete
A balanced display
She needs nothing added, nor taken away

Whenever I see her
My heart often races
Curvaceously formed in all the right places

A marvelous vision
Flawlessly made
Her elegant brilliance shall never fade

Timeless by nature
Her charm will not cease
Possessing the grace of a fine masterpiece

Endowed with a gift
Of a resolute mind
Her will is strong yet her spirit is kind

Loving compassion
Resides within she
Magnanimous soul to the greatest degree

Heroic and valiant
She shall not expire
Her courage is endless and proven by fire

She'll not be repressed
She'll always be free
You'll not conquer beauty as noble as she

- Professor 929

Beautiful Mind

Exquisitely gracious
Poised and refined
Possessing the gift of a beautiful mind

Simply complex
Enchantingly sane
Seducing my heart with your ravishing brain

Ageless by nature
There's no need to fear
Your beauty grows greater enhanced by the years

Visually charming
Quite a distraction
A beautiful mind is your private attraction

Sharing Ideas
And abstract expressions
Debates about art and higher impressions

I carefully listen
To all that you say
Speaking with you is the prize of the day

Mindfully musing
On lessons you've taught
Completely immersed in your marvelous thoughts

I ponder your words
To balance my view
Reflecting on notions created by you

Free adoration
My heart is inclined
Born of the love for your beautiful mind

- Professor 929

Rose

Alone in the garden
I muse in repose
I dream of my love as I gaze at a rose

Fragrant and proud
Bestowed with a grace
Petals as soft as the skin on your face

Benevolent beauty
Rose of my soul
Your love is a fortress that's rendered me whole

Aside from my God
You'll always be first
My love is a river, you'll never know thirst

For you alone
I will always be
My passion for you is as vast as the sea

The bond that we share
Cannot be undone
Intense and as hot and as bright as the sun

Incredibly precious
I shield you with care
Alone in my heart for you have no compare

I think of you fondly
And silently yearn
I sit and daydream and await your return

- Professor 929

Daydreaming

Serene and peaceful
Never distraught
Embracing my spirit in beautiful thought

You say that you love me
Without being heard
Your eyes speak to me, no need for a word

Enchanted by
Your light-hearted style
You set me on fire whenever you smile

You light up the room
No matter the place
Such radiant skin on your beautiful face

Whenever you speak
I'm moved to rejoice
Relaxed by the tone and the warmth of your voice

Our love is a blessing
Of this I am sure
Our union is spotless, unblemished and pure

I close my eyes
And silently sigh
Daydreaming of you as time passes by

- Professor 929

Free

You're the bounce in my step
And the song in my heart
Every day of my life I pray we never part

I draw closer to you
Each time my heart beats
You're the magical touch that makes me complete

You'll not be imprisoned
As free as the breeze
Your heart is unlocked for you gave me the keys

I'll not hold you captive
That's just not my way
So, I'm happy that you have decided to stay

As a man
Know that I am exclusively yours
Though my love is a castle with wide open doors

Please don't change a thing
You need to be you
Free of spirit and mind yet devoted and true

I will love you forever
You're essential to me
I won't hold you too tight 'cause' you need to be free

- Professor 929

Good Bye

You've been gone for quite a time
Seems a thousand years or more
The pain of losing you has made my heart extremely sore

Now the days are silent
For you are not around
I cry my self a river and pour my heart upon the ground

Why did you have to leave me?
Seems life is so unfair
It feels like just last week we did not have a single care

We were so very happy
Time flew by much to fast
I should have known the good times probably weren't going to last

I now you were in anguish
I had to let you be
Death came to your world to break your chains and set you free

I know you are at peace now
Though my world is filled with woe
I understand completely that it was your time to go

My face is gaunt and stoic
My eyes are all but dry
I'll not grieve any longer for I've no more tears to cry

I won't forget your smiling eyes
I won't forget your touch
I won't forget the reasons why I love you very much

I'll laugh and love again someday
Though for now I am withdrawn
I've got to keep on living guess I'd best be moving on

You know I can't replace you
You know I will not try
I'm filled with gratitude I had the chance to say good bye

- Professor 929

Good Morning

My Dearest Love, I woke up today
Just thinking of you
So I wanted to say,

Chatting with you has really been great
Made me smile for a while
With your humorous style

Learned some things about you
As we talked about life
You are warm and strong, with the sharpest insight

Hard working and honest
Determined and true
I am truly inspired by you

You have lifted my spirits
I really must say
You'll be deep in my heart as I go through the day!

- Professor 929

Take My Hand

Take my hand
And hold on tight
Believe me it's going to be alright

Together we'll make it
No matter the fight
Our hearts full of promise our future is bright

In the darkness
Our love is our light
I will keep you warm in the still of the night

If you are crying
Inside from the pain
Bathe me in tears, you need not explain

Please open your heart
And just let it rain
Always by your side and there I'll remain

Lean on me Love
I'll carry you through
I'll wrap you up tight in a love that is true

We'll make it together
We will not go wrong
I'll shield you from harm with a love that is strong

You are the one
I truly adore
I'll fight for your love. I will go to war!

I love you my dear
I will take a stand
So, open your heart and please take my hand

-Professor 929

Thaw

The heart that was broken
Has now all but healed
The love that was missing has now been revealed

A most kindred spirit
Loving and kind
I must proceed slowly with soundness of mind

A dangerous business
Relenting to love
I'll pray for the guidance I need from above

I must not misstep
On this arduous road
I must remain true to a most sacred code

The path is beset
By the pitfalls of strife
Protecting my love with my very own life

I'll keep my love safe
And hidden from view
I will remain cautious yet fearless and true

Life can be sweet
Sharing a smile
Stealing a moment to talk for a while

Gentle yet strong
Warm and giving
My love has restored my reason for living

Essence of life
Love is an art
I am taking a moment to thaw out my heart

- Professor 929

Prayer of Love

Good morning my love
It's a glorious day
I am on my knees getting ready to pray

Thanking our God
For the love that we share
Grateful to have such a woman so rare

I pray dear Father
Keep evil away
Bless my dear love as she walks through her day

Thank you for laughter
And love in my life
Thank you for peace in the midst of the strife

Thank you dear Father
For making me whole
Grateful to you for repairing my soul

I am overjoyed
For the love that I've won
I offer this prayer in the name of your son

- Professor 929

One

Alone and isolated
I have come to understand
That one woman is one woman and one man is but one man

You don't have to be alone
It's good to have a mate
You don't have to go through life in a solitary state

It's hard to win the race
When you have but just one shoe
It has occurred to me; life is much better when there's two

When you do not have a partner
You will progress, although
When you're running with your soul mate you'll help each other grow

The pressures of this world
Will try to cleave your bond
It will push you to your limits and then take you far beyond

But a sacred bond of love
Should never be undone
The two should walk together and their paths should become one

Life is but a mountain
Together you must climb
Your love must be a union that will stand the test of time

Trouble will befall you
You won't always see the sun
But you'll both survive the darkness if you live and breathe as one

- Professor 929

We

I've no want of bread
To carry me through
I'm nourished by love, but only from you

Sustained by compassion
And feelings we share
Our love is honest, decent and fair

With you in my life
I know I'll survive
I know your affection will keep me alive

The love you bestow
In ample supply
Is as warm as the sun and as vast as the sky

This world is unkind
So do guard your heart
They will try to intrude and pull us apart

I'll suffer their arrows
I shall not respond
I'll walk through the fires of hell and beyond

In know in my heart
That we will succeed
Our Father will give us the guidance that we need

With God in our life
We will not go wrong
With spirit and truth our love will grow strong

My love has a home
You must understand
I happily place my heart in your hand

- Professor 929

You

With you I have been blessed
I'll endure any test
I truly love you so

For when I'm worn and weak
It is your warmth I seek
Our love will surely grow

You are my guiding light
For your love gives me sight
To see the path ahead

You make me feel brand new
Despite what we've been through
For all the tears we've shed

My world is not complete
Without your body heat
You set my heart on fire

You truly have my heart
I pray we never part
You are my one desire

I'm glad your love I've found
To you my heart is bound
You mean the world to me

We have the gift of love
Delivered from above
For all eternity

- Professor 929

Your Love

You are on my mind
Whenever we part
Moving closer to you with each beat of my heart

I have fallen deeply
In love that is true
My inner most thoughts revolve around you

I think of your smile
And sigh with delight
My heart has been filled with a love that is right

Your love is a world
I have to explore
I contemplate deeply; I have to know more

Your unbounded passion
Is strong and sincere
Profound in its power yet lucid and clear

Possessing a strength
It just doesn't fail
It would seem that your love is no mere fairytale

Our future is bright
It shines like the sun
I have to declare that we two are now one

We've deserts to conquer
And mountains to climb
Our love will grow stronger and warmer with time

Affection is armor
That fits like a glove
I know I can make it because of your love

- Professor 929

Happy Anniversary

One year ago today it was
A most exciting day
Loving one another in a very special way

I am so deeply grateful
You have become my wife
My one and only love with whom I live a happy life

It seems as yesterday my love
We dreamed upon this bliss
Starting every morning with a warm impassioned kiss

Bonded by the love we share
We bow our heads to pray
Unified in faith and hope together we will stay

Meeting all life's challenges
I know we will withstand
Walking down the path of life together hand in hand

Happiness you are to me
My very heart is glad
Sharing every day my love the good times and the bad

Blessed are the evenings
When I see your smiling face
Serene of voice your words are overflowing with such grace

More than any man dares hope
Our passion is extreme
You are the center of my world, life has become a dream

Happy Anniversary!
I can't believe it's true
A year of laughter, joy and love, I owe it all to you

- Professor 929

Post Script

"At the end of it all
We run out of time
And now we have come to the end of this
rhyme"

Homeless, But Not Heartless

I had the distinguished honor of meeting Mr. James in Love Park in Philadelphia. At the time, Mr. James had recently been released from the hospital after recovering from injuries sustained in a vicious beating, which left him in a coma for five months. Mr. James is a pleasant man who is homeless due to financial hardship. However, he is thankful to be alive, and enjoys a good conversation and the company of others.

I met Jim at the corner of 12th and Market in Philadelphia. While I was speaking to Jim a middle-aged man of means stepped on Jim's right leg and did not even bother to offer an apology. In fact, he looked down upon Jim with contempt, as though he had just stepped in filth. He really hurt Jim's feelings. However, Jim did not dwell on the incident and we continued having our conversation. I learned much from Jim that day. This guy LOVES the Olive Garden!

I write about the homeless because they are our brothers and sister. I wish to bring attention to their plight because their plight is our plight. We are one people, after all, albeit not without our differences. It is my belief that there exists a great deal more that we do share in common, than we do not.

It is that common ground that will help us as individuals to relate to our less fortunate brothers and sisters if we let it. But will we? It would seem that arrogance, greed and calloused hearts appear to be en vogue these days. How did this happen? Since when did it become acceptable to leave the needy out in the cold? Is this what we have become? Are we ready to accept the fact that we have evolved into a society of self-centered wealth seeking drones without any compassion or a moral compass? Is the pursuit of riches all that matters anymore? Is it not written that the *love* of money is the root of all evil? Is the meaning of life merely *to get paid*?

We were once learned scholars, wise leaders, nurturing mothers and fearless freedom fighters with compassion serving the interest of the greater good. We once possessed the skill, wisdom and intestinal fortitude to solve any problem or meet any challenge. This spirit was not born out of some mere compulsory since of survival. No, the "can do", "never say die!" spirit I refer to is a nobler spirit born of righteousness, a keen since of civil awareness and civic duty. We all belong to the human race! It would seem that some of us have forgotten just what that means.

The fact of the matter is that there are homeless people all over the world. From the so-called richest regions to the poorest, homelessness is an everyday reality of life which cannot be denied. Homelessness in and of itself, is an indictment of the values that this world promotes as being the norm. If we are not careful, these values will prove to be our undoing. We are not taking care of our family. We are capable of far, far better than this!

Acknowledgements

I would be remiss if I failed to thank some very special people in my life.

Briana, you are the Sunshine which continues to warm my life. You are the very essence of understanding. Go forth and conquer.

Siani, you are a force undaunted by the prospects of adversity. I draw strength from your bravery, and joy from your wit.

Mom, Thank you for your art, patience and understanding. Your intellect is only exceeded by your capacity to love.

Renee, Thank you for the valued consul... the check is in the mail.

Angela, I am ever grateful to you for healing my body moment by moment. Continue to use your powers for good☺.

Brandi, Thank you for thawing out my heart with your beautiful mind and nurturing spirit.